We Know It Won't Snow In Abu Dhabi

REDISCOVERING CHRISTMAS

To Paul and Susan,

May the message of Christmas remain in your hearts all year long.

Cam Arensen

by Cam Arensen

ISBN: 978-9966-757-62-3

All Scripture quotations unless otherwise indicated are taken from the
English Standard Version, copyright 2001 by
Crossways, a publishing ministry of Good News Publishers.

To the members of the congregation of the
Evangelical Community Church of Abu Dhabi.
I treasure the memories of the 25 Christmases
we celebrated together.

I dedicate this book to you.

ACKNOWLEDGMENTS

Thanks to Sandy Arensen for the cover artwork. To Mike Adkins and Blake Arensen for the layout and design of this book. I also want to acknowledge Suzi Malan for proofreading help and my brother Shel Arensen for editing suggestions and both of them for encouraging me to complete this project.

Introduction

What is it about snow and Christmas? As I write this in my home in Bend, Oregon, snow is falling, adding to the two feet of snow already on the ground. It looks like we will have a white Christmas this year. For me, it will be the first one in 30 years. But then I never quite saw the connection between snow and Christmas. I grew up in East Africa, a couple degrees south of the Equator. For my brothers and me, seasonal attire consisted of shorts, t-shirts and "tackies"(tennis shoes) as we tramped through the nearby forest looking for the perfect Christmas tree. On Christmas Eve we would sit around the tree, opening presents and consuming the different Scandinavian Christmas delicacies our mother had prepared. It was Christmas. Who needed snow?

My life's journey would later take me to Alaska for 7 years. While there I came to appreciate the charm of a white Christmas with the feathery snowflakes falling and the world blanketed in white as we trudged through deep snow to sing Christmas carols in our community.

But life moved on; back to Kenya, to California, and eventually to Abu Dhabi in the United Arab Emirates, a small Arab country at the southern end of the Arabian Gulf. The climate in Abu Dhabi consists of 4 months of lovely "summer" weather (November to February) and then it gets hot! The weather at Christmas time was perfect for desert barbeques and sitting on the beach, but any thought of a white Christmas was just a dream.

I was in Abu Dhabi as the pastor of an international, English speaking church. The members of our congregation came from all over the world. They came from Asia, Africa and Australia as well as North America and Europe. Some were missing the white Christmases they were used to back home, but many others had never seen snow, let alone experienced a white Christmas. But one thing we had in common. We were all far from home and family at Christmas time.

How do you celebrate Christmas when you are separated from loved ones; from the familiar sights, sounds and smells and everything that is evocative of the season? For many of us, the church became our family; our home away from home. As a pastor, I was responsible for planning services and events that would keep the spirit of Christmas alive, and provide encouragement and emotional and spiritual nurture to those who were lonely and homesick at Christmas time. But how do you do that for such a diverse congregation; where customs, Christmas traditions, and even expectations of the weather differed so dramatically?

We did it in two ways. First we celebrated our diversity. Each year we would hold an International Carol Service. During the service, the different ethnic or national groups in the church would present a Christmas song that was unique to their culture. Some would wear national dress. Some would sing in their native language. Some would use unique musical instruments. For two hours, we would enjoy sights and sounds of Christmas from around the world.

The second thing we did was even more important. We focused on our unity. That unity was grounded in the message of Christmas which has very little to do with traditions, family, or even the weather. By focusing on the meaning of Christmas and the events which took place on that first Christmas, we discovered that we could truly celebrate Christmas anywhere, with or without family and with or without the familiar trappings of Christmas. My task as pastor was to remind us all of what we celebrate at Christmas; the birth of Jesus, the Son of God, who came to save us from our sins. And so each year I had the privilege and responsibility to bring a message that would unite us all in worship and awe as we once again celebrated the miracle of Christmas.

We used to sing a song at our International Carol Services

that became a favorite. Ian James, the worship leader for these services, was from Australia, and he adapted an Australian song (written by Lee Kernaghan) to fit our Abu Dhabi reality. The verses go like this:

There isn't any falling snow,
No sleigh bells ringing at my door,
But it still feels like Christmas time to me.

The camels standing in the shade
The traffic shimmers in the haze
But it still feels like Christmas time to me.

There's not a snowman to be found.
The country is a sandy brown,
But it still feels like Christmas time to me.

'Cause long ago a child was born
One starry night in Bethlehem
And it still feels like Christmas time to me.

The shepherds in the fields nearby
They heard the angels sing on high
And it still feels like Christmas time to me.

The wise men travelled from afar,
They brought their gifts, led by a star,
And it still feels like Christmas time to me.

And in between each verse, the congregation would belt out the chorus:

We know it won't snow in Abu Dhabi
But we still decorate our Christmas tree.
And you still can feel the magic
From the sand dunes to the sea
And it still feels like Christmas time to me.

Celebrating Christmas can be complicated, whether we live in a foreign country or in the community where we grew up; whether we are lonely or feeling stress that we have so many people clamoring for our presence and attention. It is my prayer that as you read these chapters, you will be blessed by focusing once again on the old, but ever new story. The characters in the story are fictional (well, with the exception of Ray, who is a thinly disguised self-portrait) as well as the interactions, but the lessons are based on actual messages I preached in our church in Abu Dhabi. As you read the chapters and relate to each lesson through the eyes of the fictional characters in the story, I hope that you will find that you can rediscover the magic and truly celebrate Christmas no matter where you are or what the weather is like.

CHAPTER 1

WHAT REALLY HAPPENED IN BETHLEHEM?

Jim ran his hands through his hair. It was a gesture he made whenever he felt agitated.

"I don't get it!" he said. "This whole Christmas thing. I wasn't raised in a Christian home. We had Santa Claus and reindeer and a Christmas tree. We put out milk and cookies for Santa on Christmas Eve, but I think I knew even as a kid that it was all just a big game. Now I've become a follower of Christ. I know that Christmas is meant to be a celebration of Christ's birth, but I must admit that I'm still a bit confused. What exactly are we celebrating? How should we celebrate? Why is it important?"

"Those are good questions," Ray responded, before he took another sip of coffee. "There is a lot of confusion, even among Christ's followers, about the meaning of Christmas. Of course, the better we understand the meaning of Christ's birth, the better we will be able to celebrate in a meaningful way. I'll tell you what. During my years as a pastor I preached Christmas messages every year about the meaning of Christmas. If you're interested, I can try to review some of those messages with you and see if they clear things up."

Ray looked around the circle. There were three other men beside Jim, all part of a small group that had been meeting together regularly at the local donut shop. The group was Ray's idea. He was a retired pastor, but still had a passion for discipling younger men. Jim, as his questions indicated, was a new Christian. Bill had grown up in the church. He looked a bit bored by the whole idea. Zach was a graduate student at the local university. He had been a follower of Christ since he was in high school but sometimes struggled to reconcile what he heard in church and what he was learning in his classes. Brent was the fourth member of the group. He was a new father trying to keep up with all the demands of a baby, a wife, a job. He often missed the group's get-togethers because he had so much going on, but he was an eager participant when he could make it.

"I'm in," said Zach. "I need all the help I can get to keep things straight in my head, and it seems to me that the message of Christmas is a key element."

"So am I," Brent responded. "With a son to raise, we're soon going to have to decide how to celebrate Christmas and what we want to teach him."

Bill continued to look bored, and shrugged listlessly. "Sure. Why not?" he finally said.

"Okay," Ray said. "Let's start with the first one today. Then we can take one message a week, looking at Christmas from many different angles. We have several months before Christmas, so we should be able to wrap it up in time to have a Christmas celebration at my place.

"I think I'll start with my favorite Christmas message. We are all familiar with the Christmas story. At least we think we are. But how well do we really know it? Did the events unfold the way we think they did? In our family when I was growing up, one of our traditions was reading the Christmas story. We celebrated Christmas on Christmas Eve. After we had enjoyed a traditional family supper we sat around the Christmas tree and read the Christmas story together before we opened our gifts. Because of this, the words of the accounts from Matthew and Luke became as familiar to me as any in all the Bible. But how well do we really know the story? I used to enjoy giving my congregation a quiz to test their knowledge. Do you want to try it?"

The men looked a bit uncertain. No one likes a pop quiz. Brent finally broke the silence. "Sounds interesting," he said hesitantly. The others nodded their agreement.

"It's a simple quiz with only four questions, and they're multiple choice. All you have to do is pick the best answer. Keep it in your mind and we'll discuss it when we're done. Are you ready?" Ray began to read the questions slowly, followed by the alternative answers.

When did Joseph and Mary arrive in Bethlehem?

a.) Early in the morning
b.) Late in the evening
c.) We don't know when they arrived

When they arrived they could not find a room in the inn because...

a.) The hotel would not take Visa or Mastercard
b.) The hotel was full of others also returning for the census
c.) There was no local inn

The innkeeper was...

a.) Heartless for not finding them a room
b.) Kind for letting them stay in the stable
c.) Neither because there was no innkeeper

Jesus was...

a.) Born in a manger
b. Born in a stable and placed in a manger
c.) Born in the guest room of a typical Jewish home

When they had all finished, Ray said, "Great! Let's see how you did. It's an easy quiz to grade, because I believe that the correct answer to each of the questions is 'c'."

There was a long pause. The men glanced at each other. Then looked back at Ray. "Really?" asked Bill. "That's not the story as I remember it."

"I can see that you're all looking skeptical. That doesn't match our traditional understanding of the story, does it? So let me see if I can persuade you," said Ray.

He had the men's attention now, even Bill's. They listened carefully as he began to talk.

***

For most of us, the mental picture we have of the events of the first Christmas goes something like this. Joseph arrives in Bethlehem late in the afternoon or even into the evening. He leads a donkey on which his very pregnant wife, Mary is seated. She is grimacing with the beginning of labor pains. Joseph moves through the streets of the town, from inn to inn, only to be turned away. No room! Finally in desperation he pleads with an inn-keeper. Seeing Mary's obvious distress, the man grudgingly gives permission for them to sleep in his stable with the animals. That very night, Mary goes into full labor, and alone among the animals, with only Joseph assisting, Mary gives birth to Jesus, the Son of God.

Is that relatively close to your mental picture of the events of the first Christmas? That's the image or mental picture I grew up with. It is the one reproduced in countless Christmas dramas and programs. But in 1979, Kenneth Bailey, a Middle East expert and a professor of theology, published an article in *The Theological Review* titled: "The Manger and the Inn: the Cultural Background of Luke 2:7." In the article he challenged that traditional understanding of the events. I would like to draw on his material to take another look at Luke 2 and see if the events of Jesus' birth happened quite the way we assume they did.

The traditional view hinges on two phrases in Luke 2:7: "She laid him in a manger," and "there was no place for them in the inn." The reasoning goes like this: Mangers are for feeding animals. Animals live in stables. Therefore, if Jesus was placed in a manger, it means he was born in a stable. Now that's strange. Why would Jesus be born in a stable? The answer is provided at the end of the verse: because there was no room for them in the inn. We immediately fill in the blank with our image of an inn: a local hotel. Why was there no room for them in the inn? The verse doesn't tell us, so we use our logic. Presumably it was because they got there too late in the day, and the inn was crowded with other people back for the census. There was no opportunity to make other arrangements. So they found the only shelter available which happened to be a stable.

It all seems logical. But will those two statements bear the weight of the logic we put on them? That is what Ken Bailey questions, especially in light of the cultural factors and other clues in the text.

First, let's consider the inn itself. In Jesus' time, inns were located primarily in major towns. Bethlehem was just a sleepy village of 1000 to 2000 people. Located as it was, only five miles from Jerusalem, it is unlikely that Bethlehem even had an inn as we understand the term. Even if there was an inn, the inns of the day were unsafe, dirty, and often places of immorality. On top of that, inns were used by Romans and other Gentiles; anathema to a devout Jew like Joseph. It was hardly the sort of place that he would plan to stay with his pregnant wife.

Most compelling of all is this fact. Why was Joseph going to Bethlehem? The text tells us he went to register for the census. But why Bethlehem? What was Bethlehem to him? It says in verse 3 that it was "his own town." Let me ask you: When you go back to your hometown, where do you stay? Do you stay in a hotel? I remember speaking to a Kenyan audience and asking this question. They all laughed and one man shouted out, "It would be impossible!"

Now I can see you might be mentally trying to flag me down and say: "Wait a minute! All this cultural discussion is quite interesting, but totally irrelevant. After all, the text clearly says: 'There was no room for them in the inn.' That proves it. End of discussion."

Well, not quite. Let's look more closely at the word that Luke uses. The Greek word that Luke uses here is "kataluma". Now what does that word suggest to you? Absolutely nothing, right? Fair enough. How about another question? Is this same Greek word used anywhere else in the New Testament?

In fact it is. We find it in the story of the Last Supper in Luke 22. In the account, Jesus instructs his disciples to find a place for them to share the Passover supper together. They are to find a man carrying a pitcher of water and this is what they were to say to him: "The Teacher says to you, 'Where is the guest room *(kataluma)*, where I may eat the Passover with my disciples?' And he will show you a large upper room furnished; prepare it there." (Luke 22:11-12)

The word "kataluma" is used in this passage to refer to a "guest room" in a family home; a room that was specifically used to entertain visitors. It served the same use as a formal "parlor" in many homes in America a generation ago, or even the equivalent of the "majlis" in a traditional Arab home today.

Now to be honest, I admit this does not prove the case as scholars do tell us that the word "kataluma" was also used in the literature of the day to describe an inn or place of public accommodation. But we do not have any example of such a use in the Scripture.

We might also ask another question: Is there another word in the Greek language of the original text which is clearly used to describe an inn or hotel where the public could find accommodation? In fact, there is. It is the word *pandokeion* which literally means "receiving everyone." Luke himself uses this word in the story of the Good Samaritan in Luke 10:34: After bandaging up the wounded man, the Samaritan "*set him on his own animal and brought him to an inn (pandokeion) and took care of him.*" The next verse even mentions an "innkeeper" and uses a variation of the word *pandokeion*. So Luke had another, unambiguous word he could have used if he meant "inn" in the Christmas story in chapter 2. But he chose the word "kataluma".

Now you may be mentally waving at me again saying: "Wait a minute! What about the manger? Mangers are used for feeding animals, right?" That's right.

"And animals live in stables, right?"

Not so fast. That is an assumption that we bring from our culture. But in Jesus' day and in his culture they did not use stables or separate buildings for keeping animals. Larger animals were often brought into the house at night for safety and even to provide warmth on cold evenings. Consider a floor plan for a typical Jewish home in Jesus' time. It consisted of three rooms or areas. The first area, on the ground level, was an entry area, and it was also often used to keep the larger animals at night. Several steps would then lead up to the main room or living area. There was generally no wall between these areas. Only the different levels kept them separate. Often the mangers or feeding troughs were built into the raised area. This raised, main area of the home was the one occupied by the family. It was a multi-use room: cooking, eating, and even sleeping would all take place in this area. Separate from this family room, often with a separate entrance, was the "kataluma"; the room for receiving and entertaining guests.

With these facts in mind, what really happened in Bethlehem?

Joseph is returning to his home town to register for the census. The only logical place to stay is with relatives, extended family, or friends. Remember, this was Joseph's home town! They arrive in Bethlehem. The time of day is not stated. In fact, the wording in v. 6 does not give any indication of urgency or immediacy. It simply says "while they were there." They are received and welcomed. Then as now in the Middle East, hospitality, especially to family or friends, was a deeply held cultural value. The logical place for them to stay was in the guest room (kataluma). But other guests have preceded them and the kataluma is occupied. So they stay with the rest of the family in the common living area. During their stay, the baby Jesus is born. We can assume it was a major family event with the women of the family clustered around to help. It was a normal birth with all the accompanying excitement and joy of a first-born son within the framework of an extended Jewish family: simple, earthy, humble. And the baby is laid in a manger, a natural, ready-made, sturdy little bed for an infant.

Well, I may or may not have convinced you, but let's consider the implications if this interpretation of the Christmas story is true.

In all honesty, not that much really changes. In fact, some things remain very much the same.

Jesus' birth demonstrates his humility.

Whether he was born in a stable or in a simple, peasant home, Jesus chose to be born in humble circumstances: no palaces; no silver spoons; no retinue of servants.

As 2 Corinthians 8:9 says: "For you know the grace of our Lord Jesus Christ, that though he was rich, yet for your sake he became poor, so that you by his poverty might become rich."

When Jesus took on the form of a servant, he demonstrated it first in the place and manner of his birth.

Jesus' birth demonstrates his accessibility.

When the shepherds on the hillside heard the angel's announcement they said simply: "Let's go and see." If this baby was lying in a manger, then, whether in a stable or in a simple home, it was their kind of place. It was a place where they could go and where they would be welcomed. They would be able to see for themselves.

These things remain the same. There is one point of difference I would stress if this interpretation is correct.

Jesus' birth was absolutely and incredibly normal.

I think we may miss this in the traditional stable story. It's just a bit too dramatic. There's too much thought of the darkness, the loneliness, the cruel innkeeper. Poor Mary! Poor Jesus! No room in the inn! But I would like to suggest that the Christmas story is not a drama of rejection. That would come later. This was a normal birth, in humble, simple circumstances. They were circumstances that the world could understand then, and which much of the world can still understand today. This baby was born in just the same way that countless millions of babies had been born before him and countless millions since. It was an incredible act of identification. Jesus slipped quietly and naturally into the stream of human history. Supernaturally and miraculously conceived, yet born under natural physical, cultural and sociological circumstances. It was an utterly **ordinary** birth of an utterly **extraordinary** child.

Well, I can't ultimately prove it happened that way. I hope

I haven't shaken your faith or spoiled your Christmas. If you disagree with my reasoning and still prefer the traditional interpretation as the best explanation of the text, that's fine. As I said, not that much changes because the Christmas message rests not so much on the when or the where, or even the how of the story. It rests on the "who" of the story.

"What child is this?" the carol asks. The chorus echoes back, "This, this is Christ the King!" The answer is found in Luke's account, from the lips of the angel who announced his birth to the shepherds: "For unto you is born this day in the city of David a Savior, who is Christ the Lord."

***

Ray stopped talking. There was a long, almost stunned silence.

Then Bill burst out. "You just blew my mind! I thought I knew everything there was to know about the Christmas story but you really surprised me. It's going to take a while to get my head around this one. It's so different from everything I've heard before."

The other men nodded. "Does this mean we need to burn all our Christmas cards and rewrite all our Christmas carols?" Brent asked.

Ray smiled. "I don't think we need to do anything drastic. After all, like I said, not all that much really changes. It's the who of Christmas that matters, not the how. But I enjoy using this message, because it gives us a fresh look at a story that may have become old hat and even a bit boring. Seeing the story through new and, hopefully, more culturally accurate eyes can give us a new appreciation for what it meant for the Son of God to become human; one of us."

Bill was the first to get up to leave. "I can't wait to share this with my wife. She's in charge of writing the program for the Christmas pageant at church this year. This is going to blow her mind too!"

The others laughed as Bill charged out the door, imagining the conversation that was about to happen when Bill got home.

CHAPTER 2

PROMISES KEPT

The men gathered eagerly the following week. They filled their orders for coffee and doughnuts. Ray chose his favorite apple fritter along with a cup of strong, black coffee. He had never acquired a taste for all the fancy barista coffees. Besides, the "brew of the day" was always the cheapest beverage on the menu.

"What surprises do you have in store for us today?" Bill asked. "I have to admit, I had a tough time persuading my wife about the 'alternative' Christmas story you gave us last week. But I think she's finally starting to buy in."

Ray smiled. "It does take some getting used to," he said. "Relax, not all the messages are going to be all that radical." Ray opened his Bible and continued, "For this message we are going to back up into the Old Testament."

The other men leaned in. They knew that when Ray opened his Bible, he usually had something interesting to say. Here's what he shared that day:

***

When I think about Christmas, I like to think of it as a promise kept. Or, more accurately, a series of promises kept. The first one goes back to the very first book of the Bible in the book of Genesis. It is found in Genesis 3:15. To fill in the background, this is the account of Adam and Eve and their disobedience to God's command, resulting in their being banished from the Garden. After their sin, God pronounced judgment on the Serpent (the Devil) who had tempted them. Here is part of what he said:

"I will put enmity between you and the woman, and between your offspring and her offspring; he shall bruise your head, and you shall bruise his heel."

Now, I will admit that this may seem a bit obscure, and not something that the original readers would have been able to decipher. But looking back on it from a New Testament perspective, we can see that the first hints of Christmas are already there. The woman and her offspring. A singular offspring. "He" would overcome the Serpent by striking a lethal blow, while absorbing a painful wound himself. While spoken to the Serpent, the promise is for us. It was fulfilled when this promised offspring or seed of the woman (but not the man!) was born in Bethlehem to a young virgin.

As I said Christmas was the fulfillment of a series of promises. Here is another one, given to a man named Abraham. Abraham was known as the father of faith and the father of all who believe. God made repeated promises to him, based on faith. But here is a clear one relating to Christmas, in Genesis 22:18:

"and in your offspring shall all the nations of the earth be blessed, because you have obeyed my voice."

A descendant of Abraham would bless all the nations of the earth. The genealogy in Matthew 1 makes it clear that Jesus was a descendant of Abraham. Another promise was being fulfilled.

The story continues in promises made to Israel's greatest king, King David in 2 Samuel 7:12-13:

"When your days are fulfilled and you lie down with your fathers, I will raise up your offspring after you, who shall come from your body, and I will establish his kingdom. He shall build a house for my name, and I will establish the throne of his kingdom forever."

There is a double promise made here. One relates to David's son, Solomon who would build a temple for God. But there is a promise that Solomon's throne would be established forever. A long line of David's (and Solomon's) offspring sat on the throne. But only in Jesus would the throne be established in a kingdom that would last forever. Another promise was being fulfilled when Jesus, "Son of David" was born.

Then there were multiple promises made to the nation of

Israel through the prophets. I will just highlight a couple. In Isaiah 7:14, the prophet speaks these words:

"Therefore the Lord himself will give you a sign. Behold, the virgin shall conceive and bear a son, and shall call his name Immanuel."

These words were written 700 years before Christ was born. But in Luke 1 the story is taken up, when an angel appeared to virgin named Mary and announced to her that she was about to become pregnant – with no human father involved! God was keeping his promise.

Even in the details of Jesus' birth, promises were made and promises were kept. In Micah 5:2 the prophet wrote:

"But you, O Bethlehem Ephrathah, who are too little to be among the clans of Judah, from you shall come forth for me one who is to be ruler in Israel, whose coming forth is from of old, from ancient days."

Even in the place of Jesus' birth, promises were being kept. I've really just touched the high points. There are numerous other promises that God made which were fulfilled in the birth and life of Jesus. But that's enough for one day. When I think of Christmas, that is one of the first things that comes to my mind and which I love to celebrate. Our God is a promise keeping God. A promise to Abraham of a descendant who would bless the nations. A promise to David of a descendant who would sit on the throne of a kingdom that would last forever. A promise to the nation through the prophet Isaiah of a virgin born son who would be called "Immanuel" (more on that name in a later discussion). And a promise through the prophet Micah of a ruler who would be born in Bethlehem. These promises were made over a span of centuries, yet God kept them all. That is something marvelous. That is something worth celebrating.

***

Ray stopped talking. He took another sip of coffee and grimaced. It was cold! The others in the group looked thoughtful. Jim was the first to speak.

"I think I'm beginning to get the picture," he said, "but I think I still have a lot to learn."

The others nodded. Ray smiled. "Agreed. But there is one thing we can all keep in mind. If God kept the promises he made in the Bible about the coming of Jesus, do you think he is able to keep the promises he makes to us? See you all next week."

CHAPTER 3

MARY'S STORY

Ray was already waiting as the other men began to arrive. He was well into his first cup of coffee and there was a fresh apple fritter sitting beside his cup. Jim was the first to arrive, eager for the next discussion on Christmas. Zach and Bill arrived together. Brent was the last to enter, rather breathless and looking a bit disheveled.

"I didn't get much sleep last night," he said. "The baby wouldn't stop fussing, and it was my turn to do the night feedings. This parenting gig is hard work."

The others smiled sympathetically as they lined up to order their coffee. When everyone was settled, Ray looked around the group.

"Does anyone have any questions about our discussion last time, or anything else related to the Christmas story?" he asked.

Brent spoke up. "As a new parent, I am intrigued by Mary's place in the story. Who was she and how should we regard her now? I know some people pray to her, but we don't do that at our church. What's the deal?"

"That's an excellent question," Ray responded. "It fits nicely into the message I wanted to review with you today."

Once again Ray opened his Bible and the men leaned in eagerly as he began to talk.

***

Christmas never really starts on Christmas Day does it? In our home as we were growing up, preparations for Christmas started early in December. Mom would get out her recipe file and the Christmas baking would begin: peppernuts, spritz, krumkakka; the list of special Christmas cookies went on and on. When we boys were old enough, we were recruited into the kitchen task force as we prepared for Christmas. There were also the shopping trips to town to complete our shopping lists, and then the wrapping of the presents. Finding, cutting and then decorating the Christmas tree was always a highlight of the season as we continued to get ready for Christmas.

It was the same with the first Christmas. In a very real sense, Christmas was in the heart of God before he created the world. As we saw last time, the first promise of Christmas can be found in the third chapter of Genesis, when God promised that the "seed of the woman" would "bruise the head of the serpent" (Genesis 3:15). We are not going to go that far back in this chapter. But we will go back nine months before the first Christmas when an angel appeared to a teen-age girl in the town of Nazareth.

The Christmas story is filled with a fascinating collection of characters: faithful Zechariah and gentle Elizabeth; Joseph, with calloused hands but a tender heart, uncouth shepherds, singing angels, mysterious magi from the east, brutal King Herod, pious Simeon and faithful Anna. We have seen them portrayed in countless Christmas pageants, and we have read their stories Christmas after Christmas. Each one had a unique perspective on the events of the first Christmas.

Today we will consider the Christmas story from the perspective of the person most closely involved and most dramatically affected other than Jesus himself. That is Mary, the mother of Jesus. She has been, over the years, a figure of some mystery and even of some controversy as different branches of the Christian church have conferred different roles and attributes on her. But as we read her story there is one thing all Christians can agree on; she was a remarkable servant of the Lord. She played a key role in the fulfilling of God's plan on earth. She was a true hero of our faith. In fact, of all those involved in the events of the first Christmas, she was the one who was required to take the greatest step of faith.

Let's pick up the story in Luke 1:26-27:

"In the sixth month the angel Gabriel was sent from God

to a city of Galilee named Nazareth, to a virgin betrothed to a man whose name was Joseph, of the house of David. And the virgin's name was Mary."

These are fascinating verses because of the mixture of the human and the divine, the natural and the supernatural, the earthly and the heavenly. God sent an angel. That's the divine, the supernatural. Where did the angel go? To Nazareth, a town in Galilee, rooted in geography, precisely located on the earth's map. It is still there today. The angel went to talk to a specific person; a young woman with a name, Mary. We are told her state in life. She is a virgin, and she is engaged to be married. We are also told her fiancé's name: Joseph. We are even told his ancestry. He is a descendant of David. All of these are earthly, natural, human details. God is making contact. Heaven is preparing to come to earth. It is that mixture of the heavenly and the earthly that gives the story of Christmas its unique fascination. Nowhere is that mixture more strongly displayed than in the life and body of Mary herself.

In Mary's words and responses to the angel in Luke 1:26-38 we also find some powerful life lessons; lessons that are valuable to us today. They are lessons about faith and about the essential, fundamental life attitude required of all of us who desire to be truly effective in our service for Christ.

I would summarize these lessons this way: **True faith is believing what God says to the point of submission and obedience.**

We will take that in two sections and see how Mary sets an admirable example for us. **True faith is believing what God says.**

There is a very strong emphasis in this account of Mary and the angel on the words of God. Faith is sometimes defined as simply believing in God. This is certainly an important beginning point for faith. Hebrews 11:6 says that "whoever would draw near to God must believe that he exists."

But believing that God exists is not in and of itself Biblical faith. As James tells us in James 2:19 in the NIV version: "You believe that God exists? Good. Even the demons believe that and tremble." True faith involves more than simply believing in the existence of God. When we study Biblical faith we find that there is a very strong link between faith and the word of God; between believing in God and believing what he says. This is clearly illustrated in Mary's example.

Let's look at her interaction with the angel in Luke 1:28-29:

"And he came to her and said, 'Greetings, O favored one, the Lord is with you!' But she was greatly troubled at the saying, and tried to discern what sort of greeting this might be."

I think we can all empathize with Mary's reaction. An angel appears and says, in essence, "Congratulations!" We would all be wondering what is going on! Gabriel then continues with words that must have been absolutely overwhelming to Mary.

"And the angel said to her, 'Do not be afraid, Mary, for you have found favor with God. And behold, you will conceive in your womb and bear a son, and you shall call his name Jesus. He will be great and will be called the Son of the Most High. And the Lord God will give to him the throne of his father David, and he will reign over the house of Jacob forever, and of his kingdom there will be no end.'" (Luke 1:30-33)

What an incredible pronouncement! "Congratulations, Mary! You have been chosen to be the mother of the Messiah!"

But there is one major difficulty. Mary is a very down to earth and practical girl. She asks a very direct and practical question.

"And Mary said to the angel, 'How will this be, since I am a virgin?'" (verse 34)

The angel answers in verse 35 and gives the closest thing the Scriptures offer to an explanation of the virgin birth:

"And the angel answered her, 'The Holy Spirit will come upon you, and the power of the Most High will overshadow you; therefore the child to be born will be called holy—the Son of God.'"

Here we stand in the presence of mystery and miracle. This is the ultimate merging of the divine and the human, the supernatural with the natural. There was no human father. The

Holy Spirit would come upon her. Did she feel his presence? We do not know. The power of the Most High is described only as "overshadowing" her. And by that miraculous power of God, the egg in her womb would be fertilized, not by a human seed, but miraculously by God himself. It is the ultimate mix of the human and the divine. Something unique happened in the womb of Mary, resulting in a unique being, both human and divine. God in human flesh took up residence and began to grow in Mary's womb. The one to be born is described as "holy". Holy because he did not carry the sin nature that is the inheritance of every baby born of the seed of a human father. He will be called the Son of God in a very literal sense.

What Gabriel describes to Mary is the fulfillment of another Old Testament promise found in Isaiah 7:14

"Therefore the Lord himself will give you a sign. Behold, the virgin shall conceive and bear a son, and shall call his name Immanuel."

The word "Immanuel" simply means "God with us."

Think of the significance of what the angel has just said. "The Messiah is about to be born. He will be conceived in and born from your womb, Mary. This will happen without any sexual contact with a man. This child will not only be the Messiah. He will be called the Son of God." It is absolutely incredible!

Now, remember our earlier statement: **True faith is believing what God says.** So here is a question to consider. Would you have believed the angel's message? The angel recognizes the difficulty of his words, and gives a word of exhortation to boost Mary's faith in verse 36-37.

"And behold, your relative Elizabeth in her old age has also conceived a son, and this is the sixth month with her who was called barren. For nothing will be impossible with God."

It is so easy to say the words, "It's impossible." I am sure, under the circumstances, that it was a strong temptation to Mary. But Gabriel anticipates her objection. He first tells her how God has already done the impossible in the life of her relative, Elizabeth.

Then he adds these strong words: "For nothing will be impossible with God." I have studied this sentence in the original language. While it is clear enough in its intent, it is very difficult to translate it smoothly into English. In a literal, word for word translation it would read: "For not impossible on the side of God every word." What is not clear in most of the translations is the emphasis on the spoken and revealed word of God. This is not a generic statement about the power of God, but rather a statement that links God's power to his word. We might paraphrase it: "If God says it, he is powerful enough to do it." Or, more succinctly, "Nothing God says is impossible."

God has all power. He can do anything. But he commits his power to do what he says he will do. Biblical faith is always linked to God's words. Faith is believing that what God says he intends to do, he is able to do and he will do. Some modern faith teaching goes astray here. In what is sometimes called the "word of faith" movement, the emphasis is on our word as believers. If we say something and believe it and get others to say it and believe it with us, then God will do it. This is not the Biblical emphasis. True faith lies in believing. Believing what? God. His word. His power to do what he says he will do and to keep his promises. This is Biblical faith. This is what the angel is telling Mary. "Nothing God says is impossible. If he says it, he can do it and he will do it."

This is the essential, working end of faith for every believer. **True faith is believing what God says.** But there is another part to the theme of this message. True faith can never end with a simple theoretical affirmation. **True faith is believing what God says** *to the point of submission and obedience.*

Before we look at Mary's response, let's take a moment to look at some of the personal implications for Mary. If we were reading glibly along, so far we might conclude that everything the angel has said sounds like wonderful good news. And it is. But there is a serious down side to the angel's words. It is a very serious down side for Mary personally.

Recall her situation. She is engaged, but not yet married.

In those circumstances, what is her mind filled with? Wedding plans, her fiancé, the start of her new life as a married woman. Now she is told: "Mary you are going to get pregnant…before your wedding night!" Tell me, is this good news? Especially in a conservative, Jewish community. Even if they bypassed the extreme penalty of stoning her, the potential scandal, gossip and ostracism was very scary to contemplate. And how would Joseph, her fiancé, respond to the news?

Of course, Mary can always explain the real circumstances. Imagine her down by the village well, surrounded by the neighborhood women. "Yes, I am pregnant. But it is not what you think! You see, this angel appeared to me and he told me…" How many times do you think she tried that explanation?

We don't really know how the story played out for Mary on the social and family front, with one exception. We know from Matthew's account that when Joseph heard about her pregnancy, his compassionate response was to break off the engagement privately. We also know from Matthew's account that the same angel appeared to Joseph directly and gave him the word and set him on the right course. In so doing, I believe God did work in such a way as to ease the impact of the potential scandal on Mary and Joseph and the family. But she didn't know all that at this point in time. Which makes her words all the more remarkable. In spite of the tremendous personal risk she was assuming, her words remain a model for all faithful believers:

"And Mary said, 'Behold, I am the servant of the Lord; let it be to me according to your word.'"

Mary's response provides a wonderful model and example for every faithful believer. This is faith in action. It is first of all a statement of a relationship of submission. "I am the Lord's servant." As your servant, Lord, I am yours to command. Submission to the will of God. "Let it be to me according to your word." There is the emphasis on God's words again. **Faith is believing what God says to the point of submission and obedience.** "I submit myself in obedience to you and your word and your will for my life."

So often, if we are honest, faith breaks down here. We say we believe. We talk like we do. But there is no final step of submission and obedience, especially when that act of obedience is costly. **True faith is believing what God says to the point of submission and obedience.** It is saying, with Mary, the necessary prayer of every true, faithful servant of God: "I am the Lord's servant. Let it be to me according to your word."

One way to prepare to celebrate the Christmas season is to ask ourselves: Do we have Biblical faith? Mary's kind of faith? Maybe we can even call it "Christmas faith."

Let me suggest three possible commitments you might need to make as you get ready for Christmas in the truest sense of the words.

1. **Faith in Jesus and his identity as the Christ, the Savior.** Mary believed God's words, given to her through the angel: that the Son of God, the Savior would be born from her womb. We are asked to believe that Jesus, the Savior, was born from Mary's womb, that he lived and died as the sacrifice for our sins, and then rose from the dead. Do you believe that? I don't mean "believe" in a theoretical, nominal, "every Christian believes that" kind of way. But believing to the point of commitment and obedience where you go on your knees before God and put your faith and trust in Christ as your Savior.

2. **Submission to Jesus Christ as the Lord of your life.** To say, as Mary did, "I am your servant, Lord." This is the commitment that Paul calls for in Romans 12:1: "Therefore, I urge you, brothers, in view of God's mercy, to offer your bodies as living sacrifices, holy and pleasing to God—this is your spiritual act of worship." Mary very literally offered her body, her very womb to God for his use. Our sacrifice may be different, but we are asked to make the same unconditional offer of our lives and bodies to God for his service.

3. **A commitment to Jesus Christ as Lord of this day, this**

moment, this situation. Maybe you are struggling with a particularly difficult situation; ill health, family problems, financial struggles, work stresses. Faith is the ability to say to the Lord, "I submit to you. I trust you in this. I trust what you are doing in my life. I accept your plan. I will do whatever it is that you want me to do."

This is the exercise of faith; true faith; Biblical faith; Christmas faith. There is no better way to get ready for Christmas and to experience Christmas not only on December 25th, but all year long.

***

Ray paused. Once again, his coffee had gone cold. The other men leaned back in their chairs, looking thoughtful. Brent spoke first.

"That really brings faith down into the details of life, doesn't it?" he said. "I have been struggling recently with all the demands on me. When the baby wouldn't stop fussing last night, I really started feeling sorry for myself. I thought of you other guys probably sleeping peacefully. But I can see how I need to exercise Mary's kind of faith and recommit myself to being the kind of father Christ wants me to be even when it's tough."

Zach chimed in, "I can relate to what you're saying, Brent. I didn't get much sleep last night either. I was up late working on a paper for my philosophy class. I'm having a tough time writing what the teacher wants without compromising my faith. I was hoping for an A in the class, but I don't think I'll get it if I say what I want to say. Maybe that's my faith challenge. I didn't realize that the Christmas story could be so relevant to what's going on in our lives today."

The other men nodded.

"I can see you're all thinking. That's good. Keep it up, and I'll see you here again next week," Ray said.

CHAPTER 4

LET'S PUT THE X BACK IN XMAS!

The next week the four men were all seated, coffee mugs in hand, when Ray arrived.

"We already bought you your coffee and apple fritter," Jim said. "You're pretty predictable in your order so we figured it was a safe bet to have it waiting for you."

Ray smiled. "Thanks, guys. I just came from the dentist and my mouth's a bit sore, but I can always find a way to enjoy coffee and a fritter. So, is there anything specific about Christmas that you'd like to discuss today?"

Bill spoke up. He was getting more engaged in the discussions each week, in spite of his original apparent lack of interest. The "alternative" Christmas story had woken him up and piqued his interest in other facets of the Christmas events.

"One thing that has always bugged me is the way so many people try to celebrate Christmas without acknowledging that it has anything to do with Christ. What really irritates me is when people write Xmas on cards and displays, almost like they are deliberating X-ing him out of their celebrations."

Ray took a sip of his coffee and a bite of fritter as he gather his thoughts.

"It may surprise you, Bill, but I once preached a message titled, 'Let's Put the X Back in Xmas!'" he said.

The men looked surprised. He had their attention now. This is what he shared.

***

I remember that I started my message by asking how they liked my title. People were looking pretty puzzled and skeptical just like you men are now, so I told them this story.

I was sitting in a classroom in seminary. The professor was

lecturing. As he talked, he would turn from time to time to write things on the board. He wrote fast, he wrote big and he sometimes abbreviated words to speed things up. Every time he came to the word Christ, he wouldn't write it out. Instead he would simply write a big, sloppy looking X.

Part way through the class he was standing at the board writing, with his back to the class, and he did it again; a big X. One of the first year students suddenly burst out, "Stop doing that! Stop writing X when you mean Christ! It's as though you are trying to take Christ out of your lecture just like the world has taken Christ out of Christmas by writing Xmas."

The professor turned around. There was a long pause. Then he said, "That's not an X. That is the Greek letter "Chi". It is the first letter in the Greek word "Christos" or Christ. Writing the letter X (Chi) is not a way of leaving Christ out. It is simply a short-hand way to put Christ into a sentence."

I have remembered that ever since whenever I see the word "Xmas". It's not an X. It's a Chi. It is not a way of leaving Christ out. It is a simple way to put Christ in. A little research has shown that my professor was not alone. It wasn't the secularists who started writing Christmas this way. It was religious scholars. They didn't just use it when referring to the day of Christ's birth. Indeed, the practice of using the symbol "X" (or Chi) in place of Christ's name in religious writing has been going on among religious scholars for at least 1000 years. They didn't do it to leave Christ out. They did it to put Christ in.

That is our challenge, isn't it? Let's put the X (Chi) back in Christmas, an ancient and time-honored symbol that calls us back to the identity of the one whose birth we are celebrating.

A good place to start is by taking a look at the word itself; "Christ". In Luke 2:11 we read: "For unto you is born this day in the city of David a Savior, who is Christ the Lord."

"Christ" is not a name in the technical sense. When we say, "Jesus Christ", we are not calling Jesus by his first and second name. "Christ" (the English transliteration of the Greek word, "Christos") is his title, his role. It comes from the Greek root,

"Chrio" which means to anoint. The equivalent Old Testament (Hebrew) word is "Messiah" which refers to one who is anointed for a particular purpose or task. The people in the Old Testament who were most commonly referred to as being anointed were the kings and the priests. Saul, the first king of Israel, was anointed with oil as a symbol of his being appointed by God. When Saul failed the Lord by his disobedience, God sent Samuel to anoint David to be his new king. Throughout the Old Testament, there are other references to David and to his descendants as the anointed ones; kings of God's people, Israel. Amongst those references to David's descendants who physically sat on his throne there are also references to a more mysterious and yet future descendant of David who would sit on his throne and rule the nations forever.

There is a reference, for example, in Psalm 2:1-2:

"Why do the nations rage
and the peoples plot in vain?
The kings of the earth set themselves,
And the rulers take counsel together,
Against the Lord and against his <u>Anointed</u>." (in Hebrew, "Messiah", in Greek translations, "Christos", in English, "Christ")

The prophet Isaiah uses this same language of anointing in a powerful prophecy in Isaiah 61:1-2:

"The Spirit of the Lord God is upon me,
Because the Lord has <u>anointed</u> me
To bring good news to the poor:
He has sent me to bind up the brokenhearted,
To proclaim liberty to the captives
And the opening of the prison to those who are bound;
To proclaim the year of the Lord's favor"

These references to an anointed descendant of David had crystallized in the hearts of the Jewish people into a fervent hope that God was going to send such an Anointed One (Messiah), a king and a deliverer to set them free. Such hopes burned particularly fiercely in their hearts under the oppressive rule of the Romans. One example of such hope is found in the story of a man named Simeon. Luke describes him this way:

"Now there was a man in Jerusalem, whose name was Simeon, and this man was righteous and devout, waiting for the consolation of Israel, and the Holy Spirit was upon him. And it had been revealed to him by the Holy Spirit that he would not see death before he had seen the Lord's <u>Christ</u>. (Luke 2:25-26)

Here was a man who was waiting for Israel's deliverance. He was waiting for the Messiah, the Christ, the Anointed One. He was not alone. When John the Baptist began his preaching ministry in the wilderness of Judea, the Jewish religious authorities sent a delegation to investigate. Their first and most urgent query was, "Are you the Christ?"

When Jesus began gathering his disciples, he first met a man by the name of Andrew. After spending several hours with Jesus, Andrew rushed to find his brother Simon. Here were his first words: "We have found the Messiah." The writer then finds it necessary to translate, "which means Christ". (John 1:41)

With these Old Testament promises and expectations apparently burning in the hearts of many of God's chosen people, it is impossible to overestimate the impact of the angel's words to the shepherds on the hillside above Bethlehem: "For to you is born this day in the city of David a Savior, who is Christ the Lord." The Christ. The Messiah. The Anointed One. The King, the descendant of David for whom they had waited so long. "He's been born, right down there in that little village." No wonder they hurried to go and see "this thing that has come to pass."

So when I say let's put the X back into Xmas, it's really just another way of saying, "Let's put the Christ back into Christmas." That's the goal of all our discussions each week. It's the key to truly celebrating Christmas no matter where you are, who you are with, or what the weather is. So next time you are with someone and see a sign or a title or even a card that refers to the day as Xmas, why not say to them, "Do you know what the X stands for? Actually it's not an X at all. It's the

Greek letter "Chi" and it's the first letter of the word, Christ. X(Christ)mas is the day we celebrate his birth."

Now how do you like the title to the message?

***

"I like that!" Zach was the first to react. "I'm always looking for ways to start a discussion with my classmates about my faith. This one should arouse their curiosity and give me an opportunity to talk about Christ's identity. That really is the central question in any discussion of Christmas and what we are celebrating."

Jim was looking thoughtful. "Wow! That was rich. I didn't know that about the name or word 'Christ.' I guess I always kind of thought it was just his second name. That's going to change the way I read the whole New Testament, not just the Christmas story."

"Names are really important in the Bible and especially in the Christmas story," Ray said. "We'll explore that more next time. Meanwhile, the Novocaine the dentist gave me is wearing off. I need to get home and take some aspirin. Thanks for the coffee and apple fritter. I'll have to take the fritter home with me. I will enjoy it more when my tongue isn't numb. See you next week."

CHAPTER 5

WHAT A BEAUTIFUL NAME

The men were eager to get started. Once again, Ray was the last to arrive. His coffee and apple fritter were waiting for him.

"You promised to talk more about names and their significance to the Christmas story," Jim said. "I really want to learn more. As a new Christian, I feel like I have a lot of catching up to do."

"You're not alone," Ray said. "Even people who have been in the church for a long time don't have the significance of all the names figured out. Let's start today with a message I preached titled 'What a Beautiful Name.'"

***

What is your name? It is one of the first things we ask when we meet someone for the first time. As you know, I was a missionary in Kenya for a few years. I recall many years ago when we enrolled in a school to learn Kiswahili. In the very first lesson, the first phrase we learned to say was, "Jina lako nani?" (What is your name?) And the answer was "Jina langu ni Ray." (My name is Ray.)

Our names are important to us. The choosing and giving of names is one of the important responsibilities and privileges of parents. I remember the long discussions my wife and I had when we were awaiting the arrival of our sons. We pored over various books of names. We discussed the sound of names, the meaning of names, the connotation that different names had for us.

Different cultures have different customs for giving names. Some are expected to give the new baby the name of a certain relative; a father, a grandmother or some honored ancestor. Other cultures give a name based on some happening or event that transpired at the time of the birth. In the celebrity-infatuated culture of North America, it is amusing to notice how certain names fall in and out of favor, based on the popular culture figures of the time.

When the Son of God was born he was assigned a number of different titles, but he was given just one human name. His human parents did not choose this name for him. The name was assigned in heaven by his heavenly Father and relayed to earth by the angel Gabriel. In Luke 1:30-31: "And the angel said to her, 'Do not be afraid Mary, for you have found favor with God. And behold, you will conceive in your womb and bear a son, and you shall call his name...**Joshua**.'"

That wasn't what you were expecting, was it? But it isn't a typographical error. It is an accurate retelling of what the angel said. Names have a way of evolving as they migrate from language to language. It is fascinating to see the different forms that a name can take. The name "John" for example: John, Johan, Johanna, Johannes, Hannes, Ian and the list could go on. Yet all can be traced back to a common origin. That is what happened with the name Joshua. The Hebrew name (transliterated as Yehoshuah) migrated into Greek as Yesous.

Why is this significant? Let's go back to the accounts of Jesus' birth. The angel Gabriel made a second appearance in the story; this time to Mary's fiancé, Joseph. Husbands and wives sometimes have a hard time agreeing on the name for their baby. Heated debates may occur. Joseph and Mary faced no such dilemma. It's hard to argue with an angel, and this is what Gabriel said to Joseph: "Joseph, son of David, do not fear to take Mary as you wife, for that which is conceived in her is from the Holy Spirit. She will bear a son, and you shall call his name Jesus, for he will save his people from their sins," (Matthew 1:20-21).

The words of the angel to Joseph actually take us a step deeper. He not only announces the name, but he gives the significance of the name and its meaning. It can be easy to miss this in our English translations. To grasp the full significance of the angel's words, we need to dig into the meaning of the Hebrew name, Yehoshuah. It is a compound word, consisting of two parts. The first part, "yeho" is the first syllable of the sacred name "Yahweh". This was God's special name. It was the name he revealed to Moses when he appeared to him in the burning bush. It is a timeless form of the Hebrew verb "to be". "I am who I am," God told Moses. "This is my name forever" (Exodus 3:14-15).

The second part of the name is the Hebrew verb "shuah" which means "to save". So when we put the two parts of the name together it means "Yahweh saves." So now we are ready to understand the full meaning of the angel's words. "You shall call his name Jesus (Yesous, Yehoshuah, meaning Yahweh saves) for he will save his people…"

Now we are almost ready to understand the angel's announcement. One more piece remains. Save his people… from what? The Jews were anxiously awaiting their Messiah to save them from the oppression of Rome and all the other difficulties of human life. But where did their true dilemma lie? Where does our true dilemma lie? The angel's words complete the message: "He will save his people from their sins."

There is an anonymous poem that captures the meaning of Jesus' name and the meaning of Christmas so beautifully:

"If our greatest need had been information,
God would have sent us an educator.
If our greatest need had been technology,
God would have sent us a scientist.
If our greatest need had been money,
God would have sent us an economist.
If our greatest need had been pleasure,
God would have sent us an entertainer.
But our greatest need was for forgiveness,
so God sent us a Savior."

"Call him Jesus, for he will save his people from their sins."

Jesus. It's a beautiful name!

***

The men were all silent for a few minutes after Ray stopped talking.

"I never heard that before," Bill said. "I've heard a lot of Christmas messages, ever since I was a kid. But I never heard that about Jesus being the Greek version of the name Joshua. It really makes sense now about Jesus coming to save his people. I guess I'm really not that far ahead of you, Jim. I still have a lot to learn too."

There were murmurs of assent from the others as the group broke up, promising to meet the following week.

CHAPTER 6

MEDITATING ON CHRISTMAS FROM THE FOOT OF MT. SINAI

"Here's one thing that confuses me," Zach said. "It's how to reconcile the descriptions of God in the Old Testament with Christmas, Jesus, and the whole gospel story. It seems like in the Old Testament, God is always angry and ready to destroy people. Then in the New Testament it's all about mercy and forgiveness. It's like they're two different gods with different agendas and personalities. I know we looked at the Old Testament promises God was keeping at Christmas. But the different descriptions just don't seem to fit together. It's one of the things my friends at university bring up whenever we get into serious discussions."

The men were back at the donut shop, coffee mugs in hand, ready for another session with Ray. The other men nodded their heads in agreement.

"That bothers me too," said Brent.

"I guess I haven't read enough of the Old Testament to pick up on the issue," Jim chimed in. "But it sounds like something I'd like to get the answer to even before I discover the question."

Ray nodded thoughtfully as he took another sip of coffee. "It is confusing," he replied. "I sure don't have all the answers, but maybe one of my messages will help. One year I had been preaching from the Book of Exodus and the Israelites' escape from Egypt. We'd arrived at the part of the story that describes what happened when the nation arrived at the foot of Mt. Sinai when Christmas rolled around. It was time to preach my annual Christmas sermon. But as I began my preparation, somehow I couldn't get the images of the Exodus story out of my mind. I ended up preaching a message titled, 'Meditating on Christmas from the Foot of Mt. Sinai.' Here's what I said:

***

In Exodus 19, the people of Israel stood in awe at the foot of Mt. Sinai as the thunder rumbled and the lightning flashed and the mountain itself shook and smoked. The sound of a trumpet blast grew louder and louder as God himself came down in fire to the top of the mountain. What a sight! What a God!

Against that backdrop, I began thinking about Christmas: a young Jewish virgin; her fiancé, a carpenter with calloused hands; a newborn baby lying on a simple bed of hay; an audience of shepherds from the nearby hills.

This is what I was trying to soak in and comprehend. Are you ready for this? The clear declaration of Scripture is this: The God of Sinai is the Baby of Bethlehem! Or to say it the other way around: The Baby of Bethlehem is the God of Sinai! That little baby we sing about, "asleep on the hay", is the God of Sinai in human flesh. If we miss this truth, we have not only missed the true meaning of Christmas. We have missed the true meaning of the Bible, of human history and of life itself.

Is the Bible so clear that we can really make the connection between Mt. Sinai and the manger in Bethlehem? Consider a prophetic Scripture from Isaiah 7:14: "Therefore the Lord himself will give you a sign. Behold, the virgin shall conceive and bear a son and shall call his name Immanuel." The name Immanuel means, literally "im" – "with", "manu" – "us", "el" – "God". "With us, God." The New Testament informs us that this prophecy was fulfilled in the birth of Jesus. In Matthew 1:22-23: "All this took place to fulfill what the Lord had spoken by the prophet: 'Behold, the virgin shall conceive and bear a son, and they shall call his name Immanuel." The writer then translates for us: "which means, God with us".

But what does this phrase (God with us) mean? Isn't God always with us? After all, the Bible teaches that God is omnipresent. But this is something more; much more. The Apostle John says it this way in John 1:14: "And the Word (referring to Jesus) became flesh and dwelt among us..." In the Exodus account when God spoke his voice was so terrifying that the Israelites pleaded for him to stop speaking. Now this Word has become flesh and pitched his tent among us.

The writer of Hebrews adds this: "He (the Son) is the radiance of the glory of God and the exact imprint of his nature…" (Hebrews 1:3)

The Apostle Paul states confidently, "He is the image of the invisible God…" (Colossians 1:15) and "For in him (Christ) the whole fullness of deity dwells bodily" (Colossians 2:9).

God in a body! God in human flesh! God (all of God!!!) wrapped up in a baby! The God of Sinai is the Baby of Bethlehem! The Baby of Bethlehem is the God of Sinai! I don't know about you, but that blows me away. I can scarcely take it in. How do we reconcile the blast of the trumpet from the heights of Sinai with the vulnerable cry of the baby in the manger? Yet it is in making that link that we discover not only the magic of Christmas but the essence and uniqueness of the Christian faith.

As difficult as these two images may be to reconcile on the surface, if we meditate more deeply on this reality we will discover that the truths about God that were on display at Mt. Sinai are also on display, just below the surface, in the Christmas story.

One of the primary lessons we learn at the foot of Mt. Sinai is that the God of Sinai is **majestic in holiness**. He ordered the Israelites to wash their clothes in preparation for his coming. Then he commanded Moses to set boundary lines around the mountain and forbid the Israelites to approach under threat of immediate death! In such graphic ways, God communicated to the Israelites that there could be no mixing of that which is unclean and unholy with that which is holy.

As we think about the Christmas story with that theme in mind, we find that the holiness of God is also clearly on display. We see God carefully protecting his holiness as he slipped into human flesh. He sent his angel to a young Jewish virgin to tell her that she would conceive and bear a child who would be the Messiah. This girl asked a very obvious question in Luke 1:34: "How will this be, since I am a virgin?" Listen carefully to the angel's answer in verse 35: "The Holy Spirit will come upon you, and the power of the Most High will overshadow you; therefore the child to be born will be called holy – the Son of God."

Do you see the emphasis in those verses on the holiness of God? Do you see how carefully God worked to ensure that there would be no breach of that holiness? He even sent an angel to Joseph, Mary's fiancé, to explain it all to him so that he would take Mary as his wife to give her protection from society's wagging tongues and yet keep her a virgin until after the special child was born. This is why the doctrine of the virgin birth is so important to us as Christians. Some modern scholars may tell us that this doesn't matter, but it does! This is God, majestic in holiness, maintaining his holiness even as he became human.

The next truth about God that is clearly on display in the Exodus account is that the God of Sinai is **awesome in glory**. The thunder, the lightning, the resounding trumpet all speak to his awe-inspiring glory which so thrilled and yet terrified the Israelites.

How is this revealed in the Christmas story? Let me say very quickly that here we do detect an immediate difference. It is this stark contrast between the thunder and lightning of Sinai and the quiet, humble birth of this baby that makes it so difficult for us to comprehend the link between the God of Sinai and the Baby of Bethlehem. But the Bible does help us understand this contrast. In Philippians 2:6-7: "who, though he was in the form of God, did not count equality with God a thing to be grasped, but emptied himself…" Theologians have long debated what exactly it was that Christ emptied himself of, but all would agree that at the very least he emptied himself of the outward manifestation of his glory.

I know that is true and so apparent in the humble circumstances of Jesus' birth. But on another level as we read the Christmas story it is also apparent that the glory is just below the surface, just looking for an opportunity to break forth. Did you ever watch a young child who has been asked to keep an exciting secret? He knows he isn't supposed to say anything – but it's written all over his face; the big grin, the sparkling eyes, the almost unbearable compulsion to tell someone, anyone, the exciting news he bears. That's the impression I get from the Christmas story. The glory is being concealed, but it is like that secret that just has to come out. And the glory does break forth in certain brief flashes in the account of his birth. Nameless shepherds are watching their flocks in the field and "an angel of the Lord appeared to them, and the glory of the Lord shone around them and they were filled with great fear." (Luke 2:9) Doesn't that remind you of Sinai? After the angel delivered his message, what happened? "And suddenly there was with the angel a multitude of the heavenly host praising God and saying, 'Glory to God in the highest…'" It is as though a cloud has come across the bright sun of God's glory, but the glory is there, just waiting for the opportunity to burst forth. And it does for a brief instant before an audience of simple shepherds on the hillside.

Awesome in glory! Yes, for a time that glory was veiled, but only for a time until he finished his earthly mission. Then he was restored to glory. The God of Sinai is the Baby of Bethlehem. The Baby of Bethlehem is the God of Sinai. And he is awesome in glory! And when we see him, it will not be as a baby. It will be as the Lord of glory, and we will bow in worship before him.

There is a third truth about God that is revealed in the Exodus account. The God of Sinai is **tender in love**. Sadly, we sometimes miss this truth in our cursory reading of Exodus 19. There is a common tendency to think of the God of Sinai as an angry God; a God of harsh judgment. Yes, the God of Sinai is scary. He is not safe. He is not a tame and domesticated God. But he is a God who is tender in love. When we think of him only as harsh and angry, we are missing the whole significance of Exodus 19. In that chapter, God is coming down to enter into a covenant with his people. In many ways, it resembles a wedding ceremony as God (the bridegroom) comes down to meet his bride (the Israelites, waiting at the foot of the mountain in their freshly laundered clothing) and to exchange wedding vows. God comes down to declare to the world that he was their God and they were his special people and his treasured possession.

It is at this point that the Christmas story really comes into its own, in the revelations of the God of Sinai, the God of the Bible as a God of love. Yes, at Sinai God was revealing his love and commitment to his people. But at Bethlehem he did it in a different way. At Sinai, God came down to the top of the mountain. In Bethlehem God came down to the bottom of the mountain and stood with his people. He put on skin! He became one of us! The writer of Hebrews says this in Hebrews 2:14: "Since therefore the children share in flesh and blood, he himself likewise partook of the same things…" He then adds in Hebrews 2:17, "Therefore he had to be made like his brothers in every respect…" Jesus' act of identifying with us and becoming one of us was an act of incredible love and devotion. I love the words of the song by John Walvoord entitled "Love Was When": "Love was when God became a man, locked in time and space, without rank or place. Love was God, born of Jewish kin, just a carpenter with some fishermen…"

Tender in love. And oh, how the love of God shone through in the simple details of his humble birth. The love of God continued to shine through the life of that Jewish carpenter. When he reached out and laid his hand on the shriveled, ulcerated flesh of the leper – that was the God of Sinai, tender in love. When he opened his arms and welcomed the children to climb into his lap – that was the God of Sinai, tender in love. When he sat by the well in Samaria and struck up a conversation with a woman who was an outcast from her society because of her immoral lifestyle and offered her living water – that was the God of Sinai, tender in love.

We could go on and on. Of course it doesn't end there, does it? In the ultimate expression of love, Jesus, God in the flesh, went to the cross. The song continues: "Love was God, nailed to bleed and die, to reach and love one such as I." The God of Sinai is the Baby of Bethlehem. That means that the God of

Sinai is the Christ of Calvary. "God, nailed to bleed and die" and to be the atoning sacrifice for our sins.

Whether we stand at the foot of Mt. Sinai or beside the manger in Bethlehem or at the foot of the cross, this is the same God who changes not. He always acts in total and utter harmony with his character: **Majestic in holiness! Awesome in glory! Tender in love!** That's worth celebrating, not only at Christmas, but all year long.

***

The men sat silent for a long time.

"Wow!" said Zach finally. "That's powerful. I never saw the Sinai story in those terms before – like a wedding ceremony. And that part about God coming down to the foot of the mountain at Christmas! I'm going home to reread the Exodus story with new eyes. I'm not sure I have all the answers to convince my friends at university, but it certainly helps me put the pieces together. Once again, Christmas is a key piece to the puzzle."

"I love the way the Bible keeps connecting and reconnecting the dots. The more I study it, the more connections I see between the Old and New Testament, as well as in the different types of literature, whether it's Psalms, Historical Books, Prophets, Gospels, Epistles. The more I keep digging the more I am convinced that it articulates a single message. I don't have all the pieces to the puzzle yet myself and I still have plenty of questions, but I'm enjoying the journey," Ray said.

"And I thought I'd heard it all," said Bill. "In fact I was getting a bit bored with the Bible, but these discussions are really opening my eyes. What are we going to talk about next time?"

"I thought we'd go back and look at some more of the names used to describe the baby that was born in Bethlehem," Ray responded as he gathered up his Bible. "I'll see you all here next week."

CHAPTER 7

WHAT A GIFT!

"Here's a question." Brent was the first to speak. "I know you said we'd be talking about more names today. But I'm puzzled by the whole gift giving thing. It seems like that dominates the entire Christmas season. It's just one giant merchandising exercise. What does it have to do with the real meaning of Christmas? It's not just an academic question for me. With a new baby in the family, we're going to have to figure it out as he gets older and knows what's going on."

Ray smiled. "That's a good question, and a tough issue to handle in a family. Shopping and gift giving can certainly dominate the season and easily eclipse the real reason for our celebration. Let me try to address it while still introducing some "Christmas names" into our discussion. There's a lot to cover here, so we'll take it in two sessions."

With that, Ray picked up his Bible and opened to the Book of Isaiah. He began to speak:

***

Everyone loves to receive gifts. Gift giving was an important part of our Christmas celebrations when I was growing up. My parents both came from Scandinavian backgrounds: my mother's father came from Norway and my father's grandparents came from Sweden. We followed the Scandinavian tradition of opening our presents on Christmas Eve. For some reason, one particular Christmas stands out in my memory. I was 9 years old. We had recently moved from Tanzania to the mission station at Kijabe in Kenya. For the first time we could have a real Christmas tree, cut from the cedar forest near our home. By noon on the day of Christmas Eve, the wrapped presents were stacked high around the base of the tree.

The afternoon passed, oh so slowly, in an agony of anticipation. It seemed like all the clocks in the house had stopped. The four of us boys could not resist the temptation to pass by the living room at regular intervals, looking at the presents, peeking to see which ones had our names on them, trying to guess what was in each package. Finally evening came. We enjoyed our traditional Christmas Eve supper. Then we sat around the tree and read the Christmas story together. Only then was it time to open presents. Mom was always very strict about how we did it. We were never allowed to just jump in and each one begin tearing open his own presents. We opened them one present at a time and one person at a time, drawing out the process as long as possible. To slow us down even further, Christmas wrapping paper was hard to come by in Kenya and expensive. So we had to open each present carefully, trying not to tear the paper and folding it carefully for use in future Christmases. The slow process added to the sense of drama and we were all able to share in the joy of opening and receiving each gift. I still remember a few of the gifts I received on that long-ago Christmas Eve; a hunting knife with a black handle and two books which became my favorites (I even remember the title of one of them: **Silver Chief, Dog of the North**).

The giving and receiving of gifts can easily overwhelm and obliterate our celebration of the true meaning of Christmas, but managed correctly, it can enhance our celebration. We need to take the time to reflect on why we give gifts. We give gifts to commemorate the greatest gift of all that was given on that first Christmas. No Bible verse says it more plainly than the opening phrase of John 3:16: "For God so loved the world that he gave his only Son…" That is the gift God gave at Christmas: his only Son, his one and only Son, his unique Son.

I want to consider that gift of the Son of God as though he were the bright package, all wrapped up under the Christmas tree. Let's unwrap that package and find out what is inside. There is another passage of Scripture that talks about this wonderful gift. This one is found in the Old Testament, in the

Book of Isaiah, chapter 9 and verse 6. The verse starts this way: "For to us a child is born, to us a son is given..." This is a promise made 700 years before Jesus was born. We need to link Isaiah's prophecy and the words of John 3:16. A child will be born and a son will be given. Seven centuries later John writes to tell us that this son is the unique Son of God.

Let's open the package a little further and examine what's inside. Isaiah's prophecy goes on to say, "...and his name shall be called..." What follows are not names in the traditional sense, but titles or descriptions. Isaiah gives four names or titles for this Son to help us understand just how wonderful this gift is. Each title consists of two words. Let's explore them together.

Wonderful Counselor

The first word is "wonderful". This means more than simply remarkable or marvelous, as applicable as those adjectives are. We could actually translate this as "full of wonders". It is a Hebrew word that is frequently used in the Old Testament to describe the miraculous and the supernatural. This same word is used in Exodus to describe the miracles God did to bring his people out of slavery in Egypt. The gospel accounts of Jesus' life are full of the stories of the miracles that Jesus performed: healing the sick, giving sight to the blind, calming the storm, walking on water, even raising the dead. These were signs, supernatural works of power; they were "wonders" in the Old Testament sense of that word. Truly the Son that was given at Christmas was "wonder-full."

The second word in this descriptive title is "counselor". We must proceed a little carefully here. We tend to interpret this word according to our modern usage. It brings to our mind a psychotherapy model; someone who listens to us, sympathizes with us, comforts us and helps us feel better about ourselves. But this is not the force of the Old Testament word. The Biblical word is actually based more on a political model. It is used to describe an advisor or planner, as used in the phrase, "In a multitude of counselors there is safety."

Two other Biblical passages will help us capture the flavor of this word.

In Isaiah 14:24 we read:

"The Lord of hosts has sworn: 'As I have planned, so shall it be, and as I have purposed, so shall it stand.'"

The passage goes on in verses 26-27:

"This is the purpose that is purposed concerning the whole earth, and this is the hand that is stretched out over all the nations. For the Lord of hosts has purposed and who will annul it? His hand is stretched out, and who will turn it back?"

In each of these references, the word translated "purpose" or "purposed" is the same Hebrew word that is translated "Counselor" in Isaiah 9:6. The child that is to be born, the child that is to be given is the Planner. He is the Sovereign One. He is the One who not only makes plans, but who carries them out. When history has run its course and we step back and look at his plan for the whole world and for our individual lives in particular, we will stand in awe and marvel: What a Wonderful Planner and Counselor he is!

In the New Testament, the Apostle Paul traces God's plan for the ages through Romans 9, 10 and 11: God's plan of salvation for Jews and Gentiles alike. At the conclusion of that great text of Scripture, he steps back in awe and says this in Romans 11:33-36:

"Oh the depths of the riches and wisdom and knowledge of God! How unsearchable are his judgments and how inscrutable are his ways! For who has known the mind of the Lord or who has been his counselor? Or who has given a gift to him that he might be repaid? For from him and through him and to him are all things. To him be glory forever. Amen."

What a counselor! Unto us a child is born, unto us a son is given. His name shall be called "Wonderful Counselor". This child, this Son is not only the key ingredient in the Plan. He is the miracle working Planner!

Let's go on to consider the second title that is given to describe this Son.

Mighty God

Maybe we've become jaded and dulled to the meaning of Christmas because of its many repetitions and so we miss the shock value of this title. "For to us a child is born…and he will be called Mighty God!" God being born! God as a baby!

Once again, the vocabulary of Isaiah's prophecy is intriguing. The word "mighty" is frequently used to describe a hero or champion. This word was used to describe David's famous warriors who were renowned for their exploits on the battlefield. They were known as "David's mighty men."

Deuteronomy 10:17 uses this adjective to describe God. "For the Lord your God is God of gods and Lord of lords, the great, the mighty and the awesome God, who is not partial and takes no bribe.

Jeremiah 32:17-19 says: "Ah, Lord God! It is you who have made the heavens and the earth by your great power and by your outstretched arm! Nothing is too hard for you. You show steadfast love to thousands, but you repay the gift of fathers to their children after them, O great and mighty God, whose name is the Lord of hosts, great in counsel and mighty in deed whose eyes are open to all the ways of the children of man, rewarding each one according to his ways and according to the fruit of his deeds."

Do you see how this passage brings together the first two titles from Isaiah 9:6? He is the mighty God who is both great in counsel (same word as Isaiah 9:6) and mighty in deeds. This is the title for the Son who was given at Christmas. The nation of Israel understood that their God was mighty and his purposes were great. They could see that in their own history. But what Isaiah's prophecy declares is that this child to be born and this Son that was coming is the Wonderful Counselor and the Mighty God! This reminds us of another name that Isaiah prophesied for this child in Isaiah 7:14: "Behold the virgin shall conceive and bear a son, and shall call his name "Immanuel" (God with us).

There are two more titles in Isaiah's prophecy, which we shall consider next week. But for now let's meditate for a few minutes on the first two titles and the implications for us. Jesus is the Wonderful Counselor. As you read these words, are you in need of a counselor? I don't mean a therapist. I mean an advisor; someone who has a plan; someone who knows the way out of the mess you're in. Why not take a few minutes right now and ask Jesus (the Wonderful Counselor) to be your guide, your advisor, your counselor. And if it takes a miracle – well, he can provide that too!

He is Mighty God. Do you need a hero? Are you in need of a champion to help you fight your battles? There is nothing too hard for our Champion Jesus. Call on him for help and see what he will do.

***

"Brent, I know that doesn't fully answer your question about gift-giving and how to handle it. I think we all struggle with that and how to keep it in balance. But it helps to understand that Christmas is really about the greatest Gift of all. If we spend time at Christmas reflecting on that Gift, I don't think we'll go too wrong," Ray concluded.

"Thanks. That does help," said Brent. "And I really like the idea of the gift being Jesus, the Son of God, and especially his being a Counselor/Planner as well as a Hero. In our culture's fascination with superheroes, it's important to be reminded who the real Hero is."

"More names next week?" Jim asked.

"More names next week," Ray replied.

CHAPTER 8

MORE NAMES, MORE GIFTS

"I'm looking forward to what you have to say today," Brent said. "I really liked the perspective that our gift giving at Christmas is a way to remind us of the best gift of all; when God gave his Son."

The men were gathered for their weekly session. Fresh coffee steamed in their mugs. Apple fritters and a variety of donut choices lay on the table in front of them, waiting to be consumed.

Bill also spoke up. "What I liked about last week's lesson was how relevant Christ and Christmas is to our lives now. I hadn't seen that before. I think that's why I was becoming a bit bored with it all."

Jim added, "I'm looking forward to more names. I find them fascinating."

Ray took a swallow of coffee and a bite of his fritter. "I'm glad you're finding our discussions interesting. The names are fascinating. I think the fact that there are so many names for Christ associated with the Christmas story is a testimony to the fact that he fills so many roles in our lives that it takes a variety of names to capture them all. So let's get started."

***

Let's keep unwrapping the most wonderful Christmas gift of all. "For God so loved the world that he gave his only Son…" John 3:16 tells of the fulfillment of the Old Testament prophecy found in Isaiah 9:6: "For to us a child is born, to us a son is given…" Isaiah goes on to give us four names or titles for this child. We looked at the first two last time: Wonderful Counselor and Mighty God.

The third name or title once again contains a surprise and

a paradox. This Son will be called **The Everlasting Father.** The Son is the Father. And not just any father. Many sons, in time, become fathers. But this Son is the Everlasting Father. How can this be? How can the Son also be the Father? We are faced with a paradox and a mystery. It is the mystery of the Trinity; the three-in-one nature of God. It was Jesus himself who said, "I and the Father are one." He also told his disciples, "Anyone who has seen me has seen the Father." We cannot fully grasp it. It is the mystery and the miracle of the Incarnation; God in human flesh. "The Word became flesh and dwelt among us." The Everlasting Father is in the Son and is the Son, and he was born of a virgin and laid in a manger. No wonder the shepherds and the wise men bowed down in worship.

But let's step back from the contemplation of the miraculous nature of the Christmas event for a moment, and consider the personal implications of this title. God gave me a wonderful father. He was a gentle man, a patient man, a godly man. In 1998, my father died. But I still have a Father. Jesus, the Son who is one with the Father, is a Father to me, fulfilling all the functions of a father; of love, compassion, guidance, provision and care. I have received his Spirit, the Spirit of adoption which allows me to call him, "Abba, Father" (Romans 8:18).

Not everyone was blessed (as I was) with a good human father. Sometimes fathers may be cruel, abusive, distant or neglectful. Or fathers may be taken away by death, divorce or some other circumstance. An absent or cruel father can leave deep wounds and gaping holes in one's heart and soul. Where can one go to find healing for these wounds?

I recall an incident when the words of Scripture came alive for me in a new way. Shortly after we moved to the Middle East, I was sitting near the softball field at the school our sons attended. The school employed a Yemeni man as custodian and grounds keeper. He lived with his family in a small apartment near the softball field. That afternoon he came out of his apartment, dressed in typical Arab dress of long white robe and came striding across toward the field. A few seconds later his young three-year old son came out of the apartment, dressed in an identical little robe. He came running after his father, little legs pumping. As he passed in front of me, he opened his mouth and called out, "Abba! Abba!" I felt like an electric shock passed through me. I had goose bumps on my arms. The intimacy of that moment; the trust and yet urgent sense of need that was expressed in that little boy's cry as he struggled to catch up with his father. It brought home to me the priceless privilege that is mine to call God my father. What a wonderful gift to contemplate at Christmas time. The Son who was given is the Everlasting Father. Maybe meditating on that reality will help heal those wounds and fill those gaps.

Now for the fourth and final title. He shall be called **The Prince of Peace.**

The word "prince" means a ruler. These are difficult times in our country when many people have lost all confidence in our rulers. It is a frightening time. Where do we turn if we cannot trust our leaders? The Son who was promised in the prophecies of Isaiah and who was born in Bethlehem wears this title: "Prince, Ruler." This function is expanded in the first part of the verse: "the government shall be upon his shoulders." It is further expanded in verse 7:

"Of the increase of his government and of peace there will be no end, on the throne of David and over his kingdom to establish it and to uphold it with justice and with righteousness from this time forth and forevermore" (Isaiah 9:7).

How we long for such a kingdom and such a prince! The child who was born in Bethlehem is this promised ruler, the descendant of David who would sit on David's throne. The Magi understood this as they made their quest so many years ago. Do you remember what they asked when they arrived in Bethlehem? "Where is the one who is born king of the Jews?" (Matthew 2:2) Jesus is the king they were looking for. He is the promised prince.

But he is a special kind of Prince. He is the Prince of Peace. In the Hebrew vocabulary in which Isaiah wrote, the word is "shalom." It is a wonderful word, signifying not only the absence of war or conflict, but describing an all-inclusive state of well-being, wholeness, contentment and fulfillment. Jesus is the Prince who came to give us peace. When the angels came and sang their song to the shepherds on the hillside, they sang, "Peace on earth," because the Prince of Peace had come.

So why is there still so little "peace on earth" today? When we think of peace, we usually think first of peace with other people; within our families, our neighborhoods, our communities, our nation, and even the importance of peace between nations. Yet a quick look around at our world and a quick perusal of the headlines reveals a very troubling lack of peace.

The reason for the lack of peace between people and nations can be found by looking inward. There is a lack of peace between people because many people have no peace within themselves, no inner peace. Worries, insecurities, inner turmoil cause many to turn to medication, alcohol, addictive pursuits, all in a desperate attempt to fill the emptiness in their souls or at least anesthetize the pain.

The reason for the absence of inner peace can be traced to the lack of a more important kind of peace. We are not at peace with God. Beginning with Adam and Eve in the Garden, we have all turned away from God and rebelled against his rule and authority in our lives. We will never find true peace until we make peace with God. And how can we do that? By turning to the Prince of Peace who came to earth to provide a way to be at peace with God. As the Bible says in Romans 5:1: "Therefore, since we have been justified by faith, we have peace with God through our Lord Jesus Christ."

What a wonderful gift to contemplate at Christmas. "Unto us a child is born, unto us a Son is given...and his name shall be called **Wonderful Counselor, Mighty God, Everlasting Father, Prince of Peace**.

***

"That really hits home for me," Zach said thoughtfully, as Ray stopped talking. "My dad died when I was still in grade school. So I grew up without a father and I really missed him.

Knowing that Christ wants to be a father to me…" He stopped speaking as his throat tightened and he choked up.

"Me too," Jim added. "My parents were divorced when I was only five, and my dad moved away and started another family. Knowing that Christ is the 'Everlasting Father' reminds me that he isn't going anywhere!"

Brent was quiet for a long time, digesting what the others had said. "I like the thought of Christ as Father too," he said. "But I really resonate with his being the Prince of Peace. It speaks to me on a couple levels. Personally, I have always struggled with a lot of insecurities and anxieties. Knowing that real peace begins with peace with God gives me a solid foundation to stand on when I start to worry."

"That's great about inner or personal peace," added Bill. "But I follow the news a lot, and especially politics. Our world and our country is in a mess! It's reassuring to know that Christ is the ultimate Ruler and that he's going to come back to set the whole planet straight. Who knew that the Christ of Christmas relates to our lives and our world in so many ways? Great names! Great gifts! And it all started with a little Baby in Bethlehem!"

With that, they all finished their last swallows of coffee (donuts long since consumed) and got up to leave.

"See you all next week," Ray said, as he did likewise.

CHAPTER 9

THINKING CHRISTMAS

"Okay, here's something I struggle with," Zach said. "I always hear people talking about the 'magic of Christmas.' I guess I used to feel it as a kid sometimes, but as an adult, I must confess that the 'magic' escapes me. I feel like a bit of a 'Scrooge' sometimes. Is there something wrong with me?"

The other men nodded. "You're not the only one," said Bill. "I remember getting really excited about Christmas when I was young. But now? Not so much! I miss that. I think the first Christmas after I left home and couldn't get home for Christmas was the hardest."

Ray took a sip of his coffee; black and strong, just the way he liked it. No 'designer' coffee for him. He nodded sympathetically. "I hear you," he responded. "This was a real issue for people in our church in the Middle East. All of them were a long way from home and the familiar at Christmas time. Here is one of the messages I preached to help them deal with those feelings, or lack of them."

***

Christmas is an emotional time of year. It is a time of year when we expect and want to feel certain feelings. Sometimes we say things like, "That really puts me into the Christmas spirit." Or we say, "I am having trouble getting into the Christmas spirit this year." What do we mean? It usually means we have captured or we are having difficulty creating or capturing those feelings that we associate with Christmas.

So what is that Christmas spirit? What are those Christmas feelings? If we could write a recipe for 'Christmas spirit' what ingredients might we include? I suppose every culture, family and individual might have a slightly different recipe, but I think there would be some common ingredients. A sample recipe might read like this.

- A dozen favorite Christmas carols
- 1 kitchen full of Christmas aromas
- 1 table full of Christmas food
- 2 cups of family Christmas traditions
- A bushel of presents
- 1 decorated Christmas tree
- Some Christmas weather (cold or hot depending on which hemisphere you come from)
- A pile of Christmas cards
- Lots of family and friends
- Stir together and add a cup of nostalgia and memories of Christmases past
- Bake and serve fresh

But here is the problem with such a recipe. What happens when some (or all) of the ingredients are missing? This was often the case for the members of our congregation in Abu Dhabi. The climate was different for many. There often were no family members around. Many people had to work on Christmas day (as a Muslim country, Christmas was not a holiday in the United Arab Emirates). And it was often difficult to find the right spices or ingredients for our favorite Christmas delicacies. How do we celebrate Christmas under these conditions?

I have always enjoyed studying the writings of the Apostle Paul in the New Testament. I wonder what Paul would say to us if we told him we were having trouble getting into the Christmas spirit? I think he might tell us that in our urgent desire to experience Christmas with our feelings, to "feel Christmas" we all too often fail to take the time to "think Christmas." I think he would tell us that the true Christmas spirit begins in our minds; with being able to understand the significance of the events we are celebrating at this time of year. It is only as we understand the significance of the Christmas events that we are able to celebrate appropriately and meaningfully. And thinking Christmas is something we can do anywhere, regardless of our circumstances.

So, if thinking rightly about Christmas is the key to the matter, how do we "think Christmas?" What does Paul have to say to us about the birth of Christ?

Let me make an initial observation. Paul does not have a great deal to say about the actual events of the first Christmas. It appears that Paul took for granted that his readers knew the story and the facts of Christ's birth. Paul does not even have any one major passage on the meaning of Christmas. He makes numerous passing references, but there is no one "in depth" exposition. Yet we can still learn a great deal by looking at these different references.

We can summarize Paul's "theology of Christmas" with four statements. (By the way, when I refer to Paul's theology of Christmas, I am not implying that it originated with him, or that his theology differed from the other writers. Paul wrote, as did the other Biblical writers, under the inspiration of the Holy Spirit, so that his words are God's words revealing God's truth.)

1. Christ existed prior to his birth in Bethlehem.

The birth event in Bethlehem was not the beginning of Christ's existence. He had a pre-existence. We see this plainly in the words Paul uses about Jesus' birth sprinkled through his writings:

"God sent his Son…" (Galatians 4:4)

"Christ Jesus came into the world…" (1 Timothy 1:15)

These are not the normal words we use in speaking of a birth. Yet his is how Paul thought about Jesus' birth and how he presented it; not as a beginning, but as a sending, a giving, an arrival of one who already existed.

2. Jesus Christ is Divine.

Paul refers to Jesus repeatedly as the "Son of God."

"The gospel he (God) promised beforehand…regarding his Son…who was declared with power to be the Son of God…" (Romans 1:3-4)

"But when the time had fully come, God sent his Son…" (Galatians 4:4)

"But he who did not spare his own Son…" (Romans 8:32)

These references speak to more than Jesus' virgin birth. Jesus was the Son of God before he was conceived in the virgin's womb. Paul's references speak of God sending his Son. In other words, he was already God's Son before he was sent to earth. Jesus, by his eternal identity has always been the Son of God.

Let's consider two more of Paul's statement on this subject.

"Who, being in very nature God, did not consider equality with God something to be grasped, but made himself nothing, taking the very nature of a servant and being made in human likeness…" (Philippians 2:6-7, NIV, 1980's edition)

Christ existed as God. That is his eternal state. He was and is divine.

"For in Christ all the fullness of the Deity lives in bodily form…" (Colossians 2:9). He is fully God.

The Bible clearly declares the Deity, the Divine nature of Christ, the Son of God. But it also declares something else.

3. Jesus Christ is human.

In Romans 1:3-4, we read, "The gospel he promised beforehand…regarding his Son, who as to his human nature was a descendant of David, and who was declared with power to the Son of God…"

Did you see that? "As to his human nature…" Jesus was human.

Let's look at Philippians 2 again:

"Who, being in very nature God, did not consider equality with God something to be grasped (or clung to), but made himself nothing, taking the very nature of a servant and being made in human likeness…" (Philippians 2:6-7)

It's there in Colossians 2:9 as well: "For in Christ all the fullness of the Deity lives in bodily form…" He was God become a man.

Galatians 4:4 says it carefully: "But when the time had

fully come, God sent his Son, born of a woman, born under law, to redeem those under law." This passage is exquisitely crafted to describe the reality of his virgin birth and the truth of his humanity: "born of a woman" yet with God as his Father.

1 Timothy 2:5-6 states it clearly: "For there is one God and one mediator between God and men, the man Christ Jesus, who gave himself as a ransom for all men."

In these references, Paul clearly declares the humanity of Jesus Christ. And it is precisely here, in these clear declarations, that the mystery and magic of Christmas lies. Jesus was born. Who was he? Was he God? Yes. Was he human? Yes. He was (and is) the perfect God-man; fully human yet fully God. He became flesh and dwelt among us. The miracle of the incarnation. This is the magic, the endless fascination of the Christmas event; God clothing himself with human flesh and becoming fully human without ceasing to be fully God.

But we cannot stop here. Paul never looked at the miracle of the incarnation without looking beyond it to it purpose. Why was Christ born? Why did God become a man? Was this just 'special effects' to show he could do it? What was the purpose of the incarnation? What was the ultimate intent behind the Christmas event?

4. Jesus Christ came to save us from our sins.

Let's go back to Galatians 4:4: "But when the time had full come, God sent his Son, born of a woman, born under law, to redeem those under law…"

God sent his Son for a purpose and that purpose was to redeem those under the law. In Paul's writings, he makes it clear that the human race was not only under the law's requirements, but under its condemnation because of our failure to meet the law's righteous demands.

Romans 8:3 says "…God did this by sending his own Son in the likeness of sinful man to be a sin offering."

1 Timothy 1:15 tells us, "Christ Jesus came into the world to save sinners…" That's pretty clear, isn't it? That is why he came.

1 Timothy 2:5-6 says it in a slightly different way. "For there is one God and one mediator between God and men, the man Christ Jesus, who gave himself as a ransom for all men..."

Jesus came as mediator. This is why he had to become a man: so he could serve as the go-between, the mediator. But he did more than that. As the mediator, he also gave himself as a ransom. His death was the price he paid to set us free.

We will never understand the significance of Christmas, or be able to celebrate it appropriately until we understand the purpose of his coming. Why was he born? Why did he come? He came to die; to give his life as a ransom, to redeem us, to be a sin offering, to interpose himself between God and man as Mediator. The events of Jesus' birth will ultimately lose their true significance, their true meaning unless we understand them in the light of Jesus' death. When we "think Christmas" we must think not only of the manger, but also of the cross.

You see, underlying a Biblical theology of Christmas is the Bible's theology of the sinfulness of man. The doctrine of the incarnation is superimposed over the Bible's teaching concerning man's depravity.

"For all have sinned and come short of the glory of God." (Romans 3:23).

Or as Paul writes, quoting from the Old Testament: "There is none righteous, not even one. There is none who understands. There is no one who seeks for God. All have turned aside. Together they have become useless. There is none who does good. There is not even one." (Romans 3:10-12).

We are all sinners. We are all under God's righteous judgment. Without this understanding, we will never understand Christmas. "Christ Jesus came into the world to save sinners." That means me. That means you. That is the message of Christmas.

There is another verse that puts the meaning of Christmas in different words. "For you know the grace of our Lord Jesus Christ, that though he was rich, yet for your sakes he became poor, so that you through his poverty might become rich." (2 Corinthians 8:9)

This is a beautiful summary of the meaning of Christmas. The Lord Jesus was rich beyond imagining. All of heaven was his. Yet for our sakes he left that all behind to be born in Bethlehem. Why? So that, through his poverty we might become rich. So that we might become heirs to all of heaven's riches. When we understand this we can say with Paul, "Thanks be to God for his indescribable gift." (2 Corinthians 9:13)

The world tries desperately to capture the **feelings** of Christmas while ignoring the **theology** of Christmas. It is no wonder it all ends up in such a muddle. My challenge to us is this: Let's think Christmas. Let's start by focusing on the meaning of Christmas. Jesus Christ came into the world. Why? To save sinners. When we start by "thinking Christmas" we will be able to celebrate with the true Christmas spirit, wherever we are.

***

Ray paused. "I know it may seem like I keep beating the same drum, but until we focus on the meaning of the events we celebrate at Christmas, we'll never get it right. Warm, fuzzy feelings we equate with the 'Christmas spirit' will come and go, depending on circumstances. But the meaning of Christmas doesn't change. The truths of Christ's incarnation, life, death and resurrection make up what we call the gospel. That's worth celebrating all year long."

"I get it," Jim said. "We have to 'think Christmas' before we can 'feel Christmas.' Once again, you've given us a lot to think about, Ray. Thanks. We really do appreciate you taking the time to meet with us every week. There are only a few weeks left until Christmas. Will we be wrapping up in time?"

"It depends on how many more questions you all have," responded Ray. "But I think we'll make it. See you next week."

CHAPTER 10

GOD SHOWED HIS LOVE

The men arrived one by one, each one taking time to shake the snow off their coats and stamp their boots before entering the donut shop.

"Brrr! It's cold out there!" Brent said, as the last to arrive. "It looks like we'll have a white Christmas for sure. Unless of course we get one of our December warm spells and it all melts before Christmas gets here."

"Yeah," Zach agreed. "I know we talked last time about thinking Christmas before we could feel Christmas, but I must admit that snow on the ground makes it easier to feel Christmas."

"I guess that depends on what part of the world you grew up in," Ray said. "As you know, I grew up in Africa. No white Christmases there. Our church in Abu Dhabi had people from all over the world. Many of them came from the tropics or "down under" where December falls in the middle of their summer. Snow wasn't part of the equation, but we celebrated anyway."

"That raises another question for me," Bill jumped into the conversation. "Why do people celebrate Christmas? I mean, people who don't follow Christ. I guess I don't get that. And if they are celebrating, what can we do to point them to the true meaning of the season?

"Good question," Ray responded. "Let me see if I can address that."

***

Why do you celebrate Christmas? I once asked an atheist friend that question. He answered, "Because it's fun!" He equated his celebration of Christmas with his celebration of

Halloween: "I don't have to believe in ghosts to dress up and have fun at Halloween, and I don't have to believe in Jesus to celebrate and have fun at Christmas."

Logical, I suppose, but sad. Every year the world dresses up and throws a big party and fails to invite the guest of honor. But back to my question. Why do *you* celebrate Christmas? Is it just because it's fun? A great deal of clutter has accumulated around Christmas over the centuries and the generations. Santa Claus and reindeer, Christmas lights and Christmas trees, Christmas cookies, family gatherings, lots of eating and lots of shopping. While most of the clutter is harmless and, yes, just good fun, there is a genuine risk that, even as followers of Christ, we may forget the true meaning of our celebrations. We throw a party, but **ignore the guest of honor.**

I would like to examine a single verse of the Bible that strips away all the clutter and states in simple words the real meaning of Christmas. I have two reasons for doing this. One is to help us as Christ's followers to keep our Christmas celebrations clear and focused; to be sure that we don't forget the true "reason for the season." The other is to give us a simple and concise way of sharing with our friends, neighbors and colleagues what Christmas means and why we are celebrating.

The verse is found in 1 John 4:9. I am quoting from the New International Version (1980s edition) because it says it most simply: "This is how God showed his love among us. He sent his one and only Son into the world that we might live through him."

Let's examine this verse phrase by phrase. "This is how God showed his love among us."

Christmas is about love. Every human being is born with a deep longing to be loved. We are born asking the question: Does anyone love me? Have you ever held a new born baby? Hold him/her close. Look into the baby's eyes. He or she wants to know, on a very basic and fundamental level: Does anyone love me? We spend the rest of our lives looking for the answer to that question. We spend our lives looking for love. Sometimes we look for love in the wrong places. Often we look for it in the wrong way. But we are always looking for someone to love us and to truly care about us.

God is the only one who offers us the kind of unconditional love that we all so desperately need. In this same paragraph in 1 John 4, the love of God is mentioned again and again. In verse 16, we are told that, "God is love." Verse 19 tells us that, "We love because he first loved us." Over and over in the Bible God says to us, "I love you."

But God doesn't just say he loves us. He showed it. Let's look at the phrase again: "This is how God showed his love among us…" The word 'showed' means to demonstrate; to make visible or known something that has been hidden or unknown. We all want to be loved. What's more, we want that love to be visible. We want the ones who love us to show it. Otherwise, how will we know? Words are good, but actions speak louder than words. How do we know God loves us? "This is how God showed his love…" At Christmas, God showed his love. How did he do that? The next phrase in the verse answers that question.

"He sent his one and only Son into the world…"

This is the event we celebrate at Christmas. That word "sent" is very significant. Ordinary babies aren't sent. An ordinary baby begins his or her existence at the moment of conception in the womb. We may speak of the baby "arriving" but that just refers to the birth event and the "arrival" of the baby from the womb into the world. Jesus was "sent". At Christmas we celebrate the fact that "God sent his Son into the world." You see, Jesus already existed before he was conceived in Mary's womb and before he was born. In the opening words of John's gospel, we read the words: "In the beginning was the Word (referring to Jesus) and the Word was with God and the Word was God." The Son existed as the Word from the very beginning.

Jesus prayed in John 17:5: "And now Father, glorify me in your presence with the glory I had with you before the world began."

The Father and the Son (and the Holy Spirit) existed in

eternal oneness and fellowship, enjoying the glories of heaven (or should I say, enjoying one another's glory in heaven). There is a wonderful mystery here, this eternal existence of the Son of God and his oneness with the Father. But at Christmas, a very significant event took place; the Father sent his one and only Son, his unique Son into the world.

Christmas is a time when families like to be together. Planes, trains and buses are always full at Christmas time as people try to make it "home for Christmas." But on the first Christmas, God the Father sent his only Son away. He sent him from heaven into the world. And he did it to show how much he loved us. "This is how God showed his love among us. He sent his one and only Son into the world."

John 3:16 teaches us the same wonderful truth. "For God so loved the world that he gave his one and only Son…"

We give gifts to show our love. God loved us so much that he gave us the most precious thing he had: his only Son. This is why gift giving has become a tradition among many Christians. We give gifts to each other to show love to each other. But it is ultimately a way to remember the greatest gift of all. God gave us his Son. At Christmas, he "sent him into the world."

We have one more phrase to explore. "That we might live through him."

We said earlier that we are all born with a thirst and hunger for love. We are also born with a thirst and hunger for life; not just existence, but real life; life that has meaning and purpose. Jesus came into the world to give us that kind of life. He said in John 10:10, "I have come that they may have life and have it to the full." Full life. Abundant life. We all crave it. Jesus came to give it to us.

We may ask: Why did God need to send his Son into the world so that we might live? Aren't we already alive?

It is important to distinguish between two kinds of life: physical life and spiritual life. Yes, all of us have physical life. But do we have spiritual life? This is what God says in Ephesians 2:1: "As for you, you were dead in your transgressions and sins."

According to the Bible, every human being is born physically alive, but spiritually dead. We are born with a sin nature, and as we grow we begin to increasingly express that sinfulness in our thoughts, words and actions. Sin can be defined as "doing what God tells us not to do and failing to do what he tells us to do." The Bible tells us in Romans 3:23 that "For all have sinned and fallen short of the glory of God."

What is more, sin has consequences. Sin separates us from God. We are separated from God now relationally, and if we die in our sins, we will be separated from God eternally. That is what Paul means when he says that we were "dead in our transgressions and our sins."

But now let us come back to our verse: "This is how God showed his love among us: He sent his one and only Son into the world that we might live through him."

God sent his Son so that we might live. The very next verse tells us the rest of the story. 1 John 4:10 says, "This is love; not that we love God but that he loved us and sent his Son as an atoning sacrifice for our sins." You see, our sins not only had consequences. They not only separated us from God, but our sins demanded a penalty. Sin has to be punished. God sent his Son to come and die in our place and to take our punishment on himself. He is the "atoning sacrifice." Because he did that, we can now have life. Real life. Spiritual life. Eternal life.

The rest of John 3:16 puts it all together. "For God so loved the world that he gave his one and only Son, that whoever believes in him shall not perish but have eternal life." An abundant life that begins now and lasts forever.

This is the true message of Christmas. "This is how God showed his love among us: He sent his one and only Son into the world that we might live through him." That's what we celebrate at Christmas time. But there is still one final step that is left to us if we want to join the celebration. That step is described in John 1:10-11:

"He was in the world, and though the world was made through him, the world did not recognize him. He came to that which was his own, but his own did not receive him."

This is the tragedy of the Christmas story. Jesus came

to his own world; the world he made. He even came to his own nation, and his own people, the Jews. But they refused to recognize him. They rejected him. Many in the world still reject him. Many people (like my atheist friend) celebrate Christmas because it's fun. But they refuse to acknowledge Jesus. That is the bad news. But here is the good news in John 1:12:

"Yet to all who received him, to those who believed in his name, he gave the right to become children of God."

So that brings us to the key question. Have you received the Christ of Christmas? Have you believed in his name as the Son of God who came into the world to be your Savior from sin? Have you received his gift of eternal life? Then and only then are you prepared to celebrate the true meaning of Christmas.

And now you should also be ready to share the message of Christmas with the people around you. Let me challenge you to commit this short verse to memory. Then you will be ready at a moment's notice to share why you celebrate Christmas.

***

"That's great!" Bill was the first to speak up. "The whole message of Christmas in one verse. I was never much good at memorizing things, but I think even I can memorize one verse; especially one as short as that."

Zach added, "That goes well with the lesson we had a few weeks ago about putting the X back in Xmas. It's also a good way to keep my own Christmas celebrations focused this year – even if the snow does melt before Christmas."

The men put their coats back on before going back out to face the cold on their way home.

CHAPTER 11

THE GREAT DIVIDE

Christmas music was playing on the sound system of the donut shop as the men arrived. *Jingle Bells* and *Rudolph the Red-nosed Reindeer* were mixed indiscriminately with *Silent Night* and *Hark, the Herald Angels Sing*.

There was a buzz of excitement in the room. The menu included a variety of flavored coffee drinks to mark the occasion. The men exchanged greetings and talked about the plans they had for the coming week of Christmas.

Ray was quiet as he listened to the chatter. He sipped his coffee (house brew, strong and black – no holiday flavored coffee for him). He took a bite of his usual apple fritter, covered with colored icing to mark the Christmas season, much to his dismay.

"What are you thinking, Ray?" Zach asked. "You look at little somber today. Aren't you happy about Christmas coming? We've talked about it enough."

Ray thought before he answered. "I am happy and I'm looking forward to celebrating with our son and his family. It's always good to see them all and share in the grandkids' excitement. But this is a time of mixed emotions for me. Especially when I see people caught up in the glitz and glamor of Christmas without a thought for the real meaning. They don't realize just what's at stake – or how significant the stakes are."

Sobered now, the men looked at each other. "What do you mean, Ray?" asked Bill.

"Let me see if I can explain. I'll start with an illustration and then we'll look at a Christmas passage that isn't quite as well known or popular as some of the others."

Ray brushed the icing off his fritter and took a bite, followed by a swallow of coffee before beginning.

***

There is an imaginary line that runs roughly north and south through North America. It is called the Continental Divide or the Great Divide. This line is the water shed for the entire continent. Every drop of rain, every snow flake which falls to the east of this line will flow east and ultimately into the Gulf of Mexico or the Atlantic Ocean. Every drop which falls west of this line will ultimately flow west into the Pacific Ocean. It is rather an amazing phenomenon when you think about it. Two drops of water falling from the same rain cloud on the same day and falling to earth only an inch or two apart; yet because they fall on different sides of this line, their destinies are so very different, ending up thousands of miles apart.

There is also a line drawn in the sands of time and of history. It is a line that divides not drops of water, but the souls of men. That line is a person. His name is Jesus. He is the Great Divide of human destinies. A man or woman's relationship with Jesus; which side of that line he/she falls on will ultimately determine his/her eternal destiny.

This reality of Jesus as the Great Divide of human hearts emerges in the Christmas story in the words of one of the lesser known characters in the story. His name was Simeon. He is described in Luke2:25 with these words: "this man was righteous and devout, waiting for the consolation of Israel, and the Holy Spirit was upon him."

Simeon was a perfect example of an Old Testament believer. He devoutly sought to live in obedience to God's commands. But more than that, he was "waiting for the consolation of Israel." In other words, his was a faith that looked forward to God fulfilling his promises to send a Redeemer and a Savior to Israel. He was waiting for Messiah to come. We are also told that "the Holy Spirit was upon him." I believe this placed Simeon in the ranks of the prophets. The Old Testament prophets are described as speaking God's words when the Holy Spirit came upon them. They received direct revelation from God through his Spirit. In Simeon's case, he had received a very specific and exciting revelation described in verse 26: "And it had been revealed to him by the Holy Spirit that he would not see death before he had seen the Lord's Christ (Messiah).

Now we can pick up the story. It is a short distance from Bethlehem to Jerusalem. On the appropriate day, Mary and Joseph brought Jesus to the temple to fulfill the requirements of the Old Testament laws and Jewish customs. On the same day, Simeon was led by the Spirit into the temple and when he saw the baby Jesus in the arms of his parents, the Spirit within him made it clear: This is the Child. This is the One you have been waiting for!

Can you imagine his emotions? I suspect his heart beat fast and his hands trembled as he gently took the baby into his arms. He first blessed God and then, under the influence of the Spirit of God he spoke these prophetic words:

"Lord, now you are letting your servant depart in peace, according to your word; for my eyes have seen your salvation that you have prepared in the presence of all people, a light for revelation to the Gentiles, and for glory to your people Israel." (Luke 2:29-32)

These truths emerge clearly from Simeon's prophecy concerning Jesus.

First, **Jesus came to provide salvation.** "My eyes have seen your salvation," Simeon said. You may recall from an earlier lesson that the name "Jesus" in its Old Testament form (Joshua) means literally, "Yahweh saves." In fact, Jesus did not simply come to provide salvation. He is God's salvation. To receive God's salvation, we must not only believe in what he did. We must believe in who he is.

Secondly, we see in Simeon's words that **Jesus' coming had significance for Gentiles (non Jews) as well as Jews.** In the words of Simeon's prophecy, the salvation (Jesus) that God sent was "prepared in the presence of all peoples, a light for revelation to the Gentiles, and for glory to your people Israel." This was radical truth for Jews who were waiting for a Jewish messiah as a national political leader. There is no ambiguity here. The salvation that Jesus came to provide is for Jew and Gentile alike.

Now Simeon turned his face toward Mary and Joseph as they stood marveling at his prophetic words. Then he spoke again, directly to Mary. Still under the influence of the Holy Spirit, he spoke these prophetic words:

"Behold, this child is appointed for the fall and rising of many in Israel, and for a sign that is opposed (and a sword will pierce through your own soul also), so that thoughts from many hearts may be revealed" (Luke 2:34-35).

A third truth that emerges from this part of Simeon's prophecy: **An individual's response to Jesus and his ministry reveals the content of his/her heart and marks the dividing line between salvation and judgment.**

These words cast the first dark shadow to fall across the announcements of Jesus' birth. So far it has been all good news. How could the birth of Messiah be anything but good news? How could there be any other response than one of rejoicing? Yet here we are told that there will be another side to his ministry, for not all would accept him or the salvation he came to offer.

"This child is appointed for the fall and rising of many…" He would become "a sign that is opposed." With these words, Simeon's prophecy revealed the conflict that would arise in Israel over Jesus' identity and his claims. There would be opposition almost from the very beginning of his public ministry. And this opposition would grow until the religious leaders accused Jesus of doing his miracles by the power of the devil. They would accuse him of blasphemy for his claims. They would seek to kill him, and they would ultimately succeed in having him nailed to a cross (piercing through Mary's very soul, as Simeon prophesied in verse 35). Jesus would be the "stumbling block" that would cause the "fall of many." And yet the cause or fault for stumbling would not lie with Jesus, but in the hearts of those who rejected him. Their response to Jesus simply revealed what was already in their hearts. By their response they became drops of water that fell on the wrong side of the Great Divide.

But there is wonderful, good news here as well. Jesus was also appointed for the "rising of many." Those who, like Simeon, were waiting for the Lord's Christ, who would recognize him, who would believe his claims and who would trust in him as the Giver of salvation. They would be the ones who fell on the right side of the Great Divide, flowing into the great ocean of God's forgiveness and salvation.

Simeon's prophecy peered 30 years into the future and on into the centuries of human history yet to come. Jesus was a controversial figure as he strode the dusty roads of Israel. He has been a controversial figure in all the years since. He remains a controversial figure today.

At Christmas, if we acknowledge the spiritual significance of the holiday at all, we gather around the manger, and marvel at the birth of a special baby. But the manger scene by itself can be misleading. It is so quiet, so peaceful, so innocent. We sing songs like *Silent Night* and *Away in a Manger* and the gentle melodies can lull us to sleep and cause us to miss the deeper, spiritual realities that are at stake. Who is this child? What do you think of him? What are the thoughts of your heart concerning him? These are the most important questions you will ever answer, for this baby is appointed as the Great Divide of human destinies. On which side of the Divide will you fall? In your response to Jesus, will you rise or will you fall?

***

Ray paused. "That's why I have such mixed feelings at Christmas time, as I see the crowds of shoppers and listen to the bright, happy, 'Winter Holidays' music. People don't realize what's at stake. I look forward to celebrating because I know what I'm celebrating. But for others who don't know or don't believe or care – well, Simeon's prophecy makes me sad for them."

"But enough of that for today," he added, more brightly. "I hope you'll all be able to come to the party at our house this weekend. No presents please! Just come with your wives, and we'll have a great evening together singing carols and reviewing the true meaning of Christmas together. I've even made some peppernuts and krumkaka from my mother's recipes."

"We'll be there," the men responded.

Before they broke up, Jim asked, "What about after Christmas? Is this it or are we going to keep meeting?"

Ray smiled. "Let's meet at least one more time. I have one final message on Christmas I want to share. Then we can talk about what we want to do after that. And maybe when we meet after Christmas they will stop putting this ridiculous icing on the apple fritters!"

The men laughed as they went out into the cold. There was still snow on the ground with more predicted. It was going to be a white Christmas.

CHAPTER 12

THE PARTY

It was snowing on Saturday night as they gathered at Ray's house for the party. Like a live scene from a Christmas card, large feathery flakes floated slowly to the ground. Ray had put up strings of colored lights on his deck, and more lights decorated a perfectly shaped evergreen tree in the yard. The sounds of Christmas carols played softly in the background amid snatches of laughter and conversation as the door opened and closed to welcome each arriving couple. Inside, the table was spread with a variety of Christmas treats, and a fire burned brightly in the fireplace.

Introductions were made, as some of the wives had not met one another. Laughter bubbled freely as the men compared the Christmas sweaters their wives had encouraged them to wear. There was food and more laughter as each one was invited to tell some story or reminiscence from Christmases past and how they celebrated Christmas growing up. The group was especially intrigued by Ray's stories of his early days growing up in Africa and decorating the branches of a thorn bush for a Christmas tree.

Ray's wife, Ruth, went to the piano and began to play softly. Ray passed out song sheets. "One of my pet peeves about Christmas carols is that we often only sing the first verse, so that's the only verse people remember," he said. "There is a lot of great theology contained in these songs, and we need all the verses to get the whole Christmas story and its significance." They began to sing, song after song: *Joy to the World, Hark! The Herald Angels Sing, O Little Town of Bethlehem, O Come, All Ye Faithful.* Several of the couples held hands as they sang.

As the sounds of the last carol faded away, Ray opened his Bible and read the familiar Christmas stories from Matthew and Luke. The men looked at each other after the Luke reading. Bill spoke up. "I see a whole different picture in my mind when you read that, after what you shared with us about the cultural background to the story."

His wife added, "That turned my mind inside out when Bill told me about that. I'm still trying to wrap my head around it. I had a tough time rewriting the Christmas pageant for church, too. Have we really had the story so wrong for so long?"

Ray smiled. "Remember, it's the who of the story, not the how that's important. As long as you had that right you were on pretty safe ground."

Brent was the next to speak. "I still have some questions. My wife and I both do, as we think about Christmases to come and our baby growing up. We've talked about the meaning of Christmas, but we haven't really discussed some of the practical stuff. How should we celebrate Christmas? Is there a right way and a wrong way?

"Great question, Brent," said Ray. "To be honest, I haven't given a lot of suggestions on that, because there are so many different traditions and backgrounds. You notice that several of the Christmas treats on our table reflect my Scandinavian background. When I make them, they remind me of my mother. She was really good at celebrating Christmas and keeping family traditions alive. We also followed the Scandinavian tradition of opening presents on Christmas Eve. That doesn't mean everyone should do it that way. A lot of the decisions you make about how to celebrate Christmas will depend on your background and family traditions. There is nothing wrong with that. It's part of the fun of Christmas. I would encourage you, as a young family, to establish your own traditions, borrowing from the ones that are meaningful to both of you and your extended families. All I would add about the 'right' way to celebrate is to make sure that at the heart of your festivities you take time to reflect on the meaning of Christmas and to be grateful for God who 'gave his Son' for us so that we could have eternal life."

"Tonight has been so perfect," Jim jumped into the

conversation. "The snow falling, the lights, the Christmas carols, good food, good friends. It reminds me of the beer commercial: 'It doesn't get any better than this.'" The others chuckled and nodded their agreement.

"I'm glad you enjoyed it," Ray said, "But that brings up another important point. What about Christmases that aren't so perfect? What if we can't create the picture perfect Christmas? We faced that during our years in the Middle East. When we first arrived there, we had to be careful about even putting up a Christmas tree so we wouldn't offend our Muslim neighbors. Things loosened up a lot during our 25 years there. But some things never changed. We never had any snow, that's for sure. We never had much family around. For lots of people in the church, Christmas wasn't even a holiday. They had to go to work! But we still had some great Christmas celebrations because we focused on the meaning of Christmas. That's what really matters. In fact, one of my best Christmas memories came from our International Carol Service. We established a tradition as a church. We ended these services by singing *Silent Night* together, and for the last verse everyone was encouraged to sing it in their own language. The melody was sweet but the lyrics came in a cacophony of sounds as people sang in Tagalog, Arabic, Swahili, Telugu, French, Spanish, and the list goes on. We were all far from home, but we knew that we were with family; our family, the family of God. That's a sweet memory.

"I guess that's my point. It's not the how or the where, or even the when that matters. It's the who and why of Christmas that gives the season its meaning. Keep that central, and God will show you how."

The evening came to a gentle close by singing *Silent Night* together. Now all the couples were holding hands. Several in the group closed their eyes as they sang. There was a long, peaceful silence as the last notes faded away.

After Ray closed with prayer, the party began to break up. Brent and his wife had to get back to their baby sitter. There were lots of hugs and more laughter as they found their coats.

"One more thing," Zach said as he buttoned his coat. "Are we meeting next week?"

"Let's wait until after New Year's Day," Ray responded. "We all have a lot going on during the holidays. How about the following Saturday? By that time, most of the Christmas goodies will be gone and I'll be needing my apple fritter fix."

With a final burst of laughter the couples went out to their cars. It was still snowing.

CHAPTER 13

GO TELL IT ON THE MOUNTAIN!

The conversation was lively as the men gathered after Christmas. There was lots of discussion as they dissected the outcomes of the various college football games from the previous week. When there was a lull in the proceedings, Zach spoke for the others, "Hey, Ray. Thanks for the Christmas party. That was a great evening. My wife and I agreed that it was the highlight of our Christmas celebrations."

The others nodded their agreement. Bill added, "Our times together really gave me a new appreciation for Christmas, and especially the Christ of Christmas. But you said you had one last lesson you wanted to share with us – even though it's after Christmas. What's up? What did you want to say?"

Ray nodded. "That's right. It's a message I preached one year on the week after Christmas." Once again he opened his Bible as he began to talk.

***

Christmas is over. The presents have been put away. The wrapping paper has been discarded (or, as in our thrifty missionary family, folded and put away for next Christmas). The Christmas tree has been stripped of its ornaments and disposed of. The last of the Christmas leftovers have been consumed.

What now? Wait for next Christmas? As boys, we would sometimes joke, "Only 364 days until Christmas!" Is that it? Or is there more to the matter?

There is a verse in the Christmas story that we sometimes overlook. It is found in the account in Luke 2 and the story of the shepherds. After the angel choir disappeared, the shepherds said to each other: "Let us go over to Bethlehem and see this thing that has happened." So they did. They "went with haste and found Mary and Joseph and the baby lying in a manger." That was their Christmas. This was no Christmas pageant with kids dressed up in bathrobes and turbans. This was the real deal; real shepherds with staffs in hand, standing around the manger and worshiping the baby the angels had told them about. The Christ, the Messiah has been born!

But what then? What did they do as they left the house and went back out into the night? Verse 17 tells us that "when they saw it, they made known the saying that had been told them concerning this child."

They made it known! That is the natural thing to do with good news, isn't it? When you hear it, when you receive it, when you see it – you make it known.

In the late 1700's, a man by the name of William Carey wrote a short tract. Its title began with the words, "An Enquiry Into the Obligations of Christians..." His little booklet became a Christian classic and served a vital role in launching the modern mission movement. In that booklet, right after the title and before the introduction is a quotation from the Book of Romans, chapter 10 beginning in verse 12:

"For there is no distinction between Jew and Greek; for the same Lord is Lord of all, bestowing his riches on all who call on him. For "everyone who calls on the name of the Lord will be saved." How then will they call on him in whom they have not believed? And how are they to believe in him of whom they have never heard? And how are they to hear without someone preaching? And how are they to preach unless they are sent?"

This was the response of the shepherds on that first Christmas. It is the natural response to the incredible words they heard from the mouth of the angel. A Savior has been born! Christ (Messiah) has been born in Bethlehem! This is good news. Good news needs to be proclaimed.

No one displayed this passion for sharing the message of Christ more than the Apostle Paul. It permeated his life and writing. We could go through passage after passage in his writings and find numerous examples. In this message we will examine a very limited sampling, taken from Paul's letter to the Romans.

The first thing we find is that the passion Paul had for sharing the good news of Jesus Christ was rooted in his deep compassion for the lost. Consider Romans 9:1-3: "I am speaking the truth in Christ—I am not lying; my conscience bears me witness in the Holy Spirit— that I have great sorrow and unceasing anguish in my heart. For I could wish that I myself were accursed and cut off from Christ for the sake of my brothers, my kinsmen according to the flesh."

These verses have often haunted me. I read that and I ask myself the question: Do I have that? Do I carry "great sorrow and unceasing anguish in my heart" for the lost people all around me? Paul says that he is not exaggerating. He is not lying. He even calls the Holy Spirit to be his witness. "Great sorrow and unceasing anguish?" Why, Paul? "Because my fellow countrymen, my kinsmen, my race, my people don't know Christ. They are lost!" Let's leave aside the technicalities of Bible interpretation for a moment and hear and feel the raw human emotion. Do you share that? Do I share that?

The final verse of this text is almost beyond belief. In verse 3, Paul says. "For I could wish that I myself were accursed and cut off from Christ for the sake of my brothers, my kinsmen according to the flesh."

Hear what Paul is saying. He uses a rare grammatical construction here that protects him from outright heresy. It is rendered, "I could wish…" He doesn't quite say that he does wish it. He says, so to speak, "I am this close! My concern for my brothers is so great that if I could exchange my salvation for theirs (and I know I can't) I am right on the point of being willing to take their place in Hell if that would lead to their salvation."

Can I say that? Do I have that same passion for the lost that I would be willing to give up my own salvation for them? And if that is too much to ask, if that is too high a bar, what am I willing to give up so that others can hear the good news of Jesus Christ and come to salvation?

This passion found a practical expression for Paul in the

form of prayer. In Romans 10:1 he says, "Brothers, my heart's desire and prayer to God for them is that they may be saved." Paul carried this burden with him into his prayer life, and he regularly and passionately prayed for the lost. In his case, he carried a special prayer burden for the Jews.

Let us pause and explore this for a moment. It is my opinion that God often gives particular prayer burdens to us as his followers. We are not all equally burdened to pray for everyone and every people group. That would be physically impossible, or render our prayers so broad and general as to be almost meaningless. But I believe we all should carry specific burdens of prayer for the lost. If you don't have that, ask God to give it to you. It may be certain individuals among your family and friends. It may also be a wider category of people or an entire people group, or a region. When my parents were in Bible college in California in the 1930s, their college was organized into "prayer bands" to pray for particular regions of the world. They both went to the prayer band for Africa. In fact, that is where they met. After marriage, they ended up spending almost 45 years in Africa, sharing the Gospel. It began with a prayer burden. Who are we praying for?

Paul's passion for the lost found expression in his prayers. But it did not stop there. When Paul compares the eternal destiny of the lost with the incredible spiritual riches on offer in Christ, it prompts him to ask a series of rhetorical questions which lead to a clear picture of our obligation as Christ's followers.

"How then will they call on him in whom they have not believed? And how are they to believe in him of whom they have never heard? And how are they to hear without someone preaching? And how are they to preach unless they are sent? As it is written, "How beautiful are the feet of those who preach the good news!" (Romans 10:14-15)

It's a perfectly logical progression, is it not? In order to experience the riches of Christ (and the Christmas story), people must call on him. In order to call on him, they have to believe in him. In order to believe in him, they have to hear about him. And how will they hear about him? Someone has to tell them! And that is our job. That is our obligation as those who have received the riches of Jesus Christ and been justified by faith.

By the way, the word "preach" here is not limited to something that happens in a church building and it does not require a pulpit or a microphone or a seminary degree. It means to serve as a herald; someone who makes an official message known by proclaiming it. The proclamation can be done before multitudes or it can be done one individual to another. It is a task for every follower of Christ. It was the task that the shepherds took up so eagerly on the first Christmas. "When they saw…they made it known."

There is one final link in this chain of responsibility. Not everyone lives within reach or sound of a Gospel preaching community. They live on the other side of some kind of barrier of geographical or cultural or linguistic distance. They will not be reached in the natural course of everyday life. Someone must go to them. That requires "sending." This is where William Carey focused his famous work. At that time, England had many churches. Anyone in England who seriously cared to find a church where the Gospel was proclaimed could do so. William Carey did not disparage the work or the Gospel preaching of those churches. But he wrote to declare that it was not enough. There were many peoples and places in the world where there was no Gospel witness. It was time, Carey argued, to be deliberate and intentional to send people to those places and to those people. I know Paul would have said a hearty "Amen!" to William Carey's writings. William Carey took his own words to heart and spent over 50 years proclaiming the Gospel in India.

This is the final challenge of the Christmas story. This is the answer to the "what now?" question. Paul says it this way in Romans 1:14: "I am under obligation both to Greeks and to barbarians, both to the wise and to the foolish." But for Paul, this was more than just a burdensome duty. Look at what follows in verse 15: "So I am eager to preach the gospel to you also." May God give us that same eagerness. Like the shepherds as they left Mary and Joseph and the baby Jesus and rushed out into the night: what they had seen, they made known.

I want to close with an illustration taken from a story in the Old Testament. The Jewish city of Samaria was under siege by the Syrian army. It was a long siege and the people of the city grew desperate. The people were starving. Then God acted. One night he caused the Syrian army to hear sounds as though a great army was advancing against them. In terror, they all fled, leaving their tents, equipment and even their horses behind.

But in the city of Samaria, the starving people were unaware of what had happened. There were four men at the gate of the city. They were afflicted with the disease of leprosy. They were outcasts and therefore even more desperate than the others. That night they decided to go out and beg for food from the Syrian army. "What do we have to lose?" they asked each other. "The worst they can do is kill us, and we are going to die of starvation anyway if we stay in the city."

So they went out to the Syrian camp. To their surprise, they found it completely deserted. They found food to eat and wine to drink. They feasted. They carried off some of the silver and gold that they found and hid it. They came back for another load of loot.

But then they had an attack of conscience as they thought of their still-starving countrymen huddled behind the city walls. This is what they said to each other: "We are not doing right. This day is a day of good news and we remain silent." (2 Kings 7:9).

In these weeks together we have been considering the good news of Christmas. But let's not turn this into a private party. That's just not right. This day is a day of good news. Let's not remain silent. In the words of the old Christmas carol: **Go tell it on the mountain, that Jesus Christ is born!**

***

Ray stopped talking and closed his Bible. "That's it," he said. "The ball is in our court now. Christmas isn't a private party. The message of Christmas is a message for the world."

The men were all silent. The mood was sober.

"That's a heavy responsibility," Bill said. "I've heard lots of missionary speakers when I was growing up in the church. I must admit, I've sometimes felt a tug on my conscience when they would describe their ministries and what God is doing overseas. I wonder if that's what God has in mind for me."

Ray nodded. "Maybe he does, Bill," he said. "But keep in mind, going to another country isn't what makes a person a missionary. If you're not sharing your faith here at home, that won't change by getting on an airplane."

Zach was next to speak. "I think I get that. As you were talking, I thought of several of my classmates at college that I've struck up a friendship with. I don't think they even know I'm a Christian. Maybe that's where I need to start."

"That's a great idea," Ray said. "I encourage all of us to ask God to show us the people we already know, in our neighborhood or at work, whom we can share with."

Jim was slower to respond. "I can understand that it's my responsibility, and you've given us a lot of great stuff to get started. But I'm still feeling rather intimidated. As a new Christian, I don't feel like I know enough. I still have a lot to learn myself before I start talking to others."

"Those are valid feelings, Jim," Ray responded. "I still feel inadequate myself a lot of times. But the Bible calls us to be a witness. A witness is simply someone who shares what he knows. It's never too soon to get started. Meanwhile, we can continue to expand our knowledge and keep learning ourselves."

"That's what I wanted to ask," Brent said. "We're done talking about Christmas. But is there any way you can keep meeting with us? I think we all have a lot more to learn." The others nodded eagerly.

"I'd love to do that," Ray replied. "I'm retired now. I've got the time if you do. What do you say we meet again next Saturday? I have some great ideas for where we might start."

CPSIA information can be obtained
at www.ICGtesting.com
Printed in the USA
JSHW020933041219
2735JS00001B/2